Moulinex MICROCHEF
EASY MICROWAVE COOKING

by Bernard & Christine Charretton

Adapted by Jane Massey

(Introduction edited by Cecilia Norman)

TÉLÉCUISINE

© TELECUISINE, Paris, 1984
ISBN 2-904343-03-2

TELECUISINE Publisher
3, rue du Marché St Honoré - 75001 PARIS

Contents

KEY TO SYMBOLS

ᵐ — Full power

ᵘ — Slow cook

ᵈ — Defrost

Introduction

Fire was man's first important discovery. He soon learnt how to light it, how to keep it going and how to control it. For thousands of years fire was the only cooking source. As time passed and other heat sources were discovered, coal produced gas and electricity, water was harnessed for hydro-electrics and oil provided a multiplicity of uses. Stoves were able to be powered by solid fuel, by electricity or gas and by oil but the cooking methods remained the same as ever. Food was still cooked either in, on or over the heat source.

It wasn't until the middle of the twentieth century that a new cooking concept was discovered — how to cook by producing heat inside the food without the need to apply direct heat. Microwaves had arrived.

There are many stories about the way that microwaves as a cooking medium were discovered, one of them being that of a physicist, Dr. Percy Spencer, who, while absorbed in his laboratory work, absent-mindedly put his sandwich on a piece of apparatus and on picking it up several minutes later, found that it was cooked right through.

In 1947 the first microwave ovens were used in hospital kitchens and military canteens. Today about 20 million homes across the world use this new appliance.

What are microwaves ?

Microwaves are not new, they are naturally present in the atmosphere around the sun and are produced during thunderstorms. They are electrical energy which has been transmitted not through wires, but through a magnetic field. This energy is similar to that utilized for the transmission of television and radio waves, long-distance telephones and radar. The number of times that microwaves change direction is known as "frequency" and is calculated in MgH. This indicates the number of times in billions per second that the microwaves change direction which is occurring all the time while a microwave oven is in operation.

	electro magnetic spectrum							
frequency (hertz)						2450 MHz 915 MHz		
wave lengths			0.01mm 1mm		0.12m 0.3m		1m 100m	
	higher radiations	x ray	ultra violet	infra-red	radar	microwaves		tv & radio

invisible light

How do microwaves cook ?

Food is made up of different components, including mineral salts, fat particles and water. Most foods have a high proportion of water and it is this which attracts the microwaves.
There is rapid vibration as these water molecules change direction towards the microwaves at a rate of 2,450 billion times per second in a domestic oven. Thus the water molecules become very excited and the friction occurring causes a considerable and rapid build-up of heat in the food itself.

This action differs from conventional cooking in that it takes place within the food and not initially on the surface. On penetration the microwaves begin to lose their strength and food more than 3 cm (1 1/2 ") thick then continues cooking by conduction.

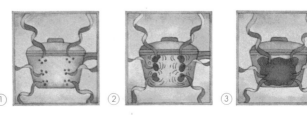

① ② ③

The construction of the microwave oven

The exterior of the appliance comprises of a metal cabinet and a door. The controls on the outside panel consist of an on/off switch, a timer dial and a selector switch. The electric current supplies the magnetron (1) which emits electro-magnetic waves. The wave-guide (2) channels the microwaves from the magnetron into the oven chamber, and on entering the chamber a stirrer (3) breaks up the microwaves so that they are evenly distributed around the oven.

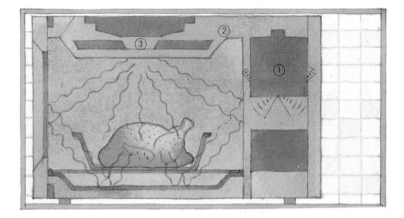

Suitable utensils

Microwaves cause a temperature rise in the food. Containers must be made of materials which permit the microwaves to pass through freely, allowing the maximum microwave power to reach the food. For this reason these containers are described as « transparent », and let the microwaves pass through as light passes through a window without affecting it. You must not use metal dishes which will reflect the waves sending them back to the walls of the oven with inevitable risk of damage. Some containers may appear to be made of pottery but have some metal in their manufacture, and these are unsuitable for microwave cooking. Other dishes possibly of the ceramic type have impurities in the materials and these may cause the dish to absorb some of the microwaves, at the same time heating the dish itself. These dishes can become very hot and you run the risk of burning yourself when picking them up. It is possible that their life will be shortened by constant microwave use. However most ceramics and pottery are ideal.

To test their suitability for microwave usage, put the empty dish into the oven beside a glass of water. Switch on the power to Maximum for one minute. If after this the dish is cold it can be said to be transparent and microwave safe. If the dish becomes hot it is « absorbent » and must not be used. If the dish feels warm to the touch it can be used for short periods.

METALS MUST NEVER BE USED IN THE MICROWAVE OVEN. NO SAUCEPANS, NO METAL MOULDS, NO SMALL TINS, NO ALUMINIUM FOIL. NOR MUST YOU USE UTENSILS WITH METAL COMPONENTS, WITH SILVER OR GOLD DESIGNS OR INSCRIPTIONS.

Fine metal such as the wire tags for sealing polythene or roaster bags must never be allowed in the microwave oven as they will spark, damage the magnetron and could set fire to their paper covering. Laminated foil butter papers can be highly dangerous.

The best materials are glass such as Pyrex, Arcopal, Vision. These resist raised temperatures as well as the low ones (you can freeze, defrost and cook in the same dish). They do not heat up (except slightly after prolonged use) and are easy to wash in the dishwasher.

Only glass which can resist high temperatures should be used in the microwave. Cheap glass goblets are usually safe for very short periods, but lead crystal or any glass with a metal content would naturally be unsuitable and dangerous.

China and porcelain are suitable for microwave usage provided they have no metallic designs, and results will vary according to composition and thickness. Fine china should be tested before use. While most earthenware and pottery is suitable, unglazed earthenware must be avoided because it is porous.

Paper based dishes must be used carefully. These are inflammable and must not be submitted to high temperatures or used for prolonged cooking. Kitchen paper can catch fire if it becomes over-dry, but when there is moisture present in the cooking and there is no fat or sugar placed directly against the paper, burning is unlikely. Greaseproof paper can be used to cover dishes during cooking.

Some plastics are suitable for microwave cooking and there is a range specially designed for the purpose. Rigid or semi-rigid plastics may be used for reheating but the foods contained in them must not reach high temperatures, and fats or sugar will cause scarring and possibly cause holes to appear in the base and corners of these dishes.

Plastic cling film can be used to cover foods but remember to make a hole in the centre or pull back one corner to allow steam to escape.

Many dishes are now being marked as microwave proof or microwave suitable. Always follow the manufacturer's instructions.

Browning dishes specially designed for the microwave oven can be used to cook and to brown food. The principle is explained in pictures a little further on.

Choose the right sized containers or dishes to fit the quantity of food being cooked. For best results they should neither be too large nor too small.

Short cuts and tips

There are so many uses for the microwave oven. For example you can use it to soften hard butter or melt chocolate when making desserts. It can be used for drying herbs or putting the freshness back into stale cakes. Babies' feeding bottles can be frequently prepared. Microwaves allow you to heat up water in a few seconds. To reheat baby foods, remove the metal lids from glass jars and replace with plastic cling film. Reheat for a few seconds, then stir thoroughly and test before offering the food to the baby.

Young children can prepare drinks and cooked dishes in a microwave oven, very safely and within seconds.

What does a microwave oven do ?

It will cook, reheat and defrost, and within these capabilities it can refresh bread, melt chocolate and cope with many small culinary chores.

Getting the best out of your microwave.

To make the best use of you microwave oven you must forget some of the conventional cooking methods, adapt others and acquire a few new ones. In keeping with all cookery skills you must give yourself a little time to adapt to slightly different methods of cooking. An understanding of the principles involved will help you to produce dishes quickly and successfully.

Cooking

Choose good quality fresh food as microwaves have little or no effect on the flavours. Because of the speed of cooking, ingredients remain at their best and the colour is retained.

Add less seasoning since you will be cooking in less liquid. You can always adjust this after cooking if you feel it necessary.

High water content foods such as apples and spinach will cook quicker than dry foods but many foods do require some added liquid. This may be water, stock, wine or vinegar. Add these liquids sparingly because there is much less evaporation during microwave cooking, and cooking will also be faster when less liquid needs to be heated and activated.

Try to select evenly-shaped pieces but if this is not possible, arrange thicker or larger pieces around the outside of the dish.

Although you can cook three different items at one time, because of their various densities, you will find that some cook more quickly than others. At first you will find it best to cook only one type of food at a time.

Prick food such as potatoes, sausages, tomatoes and all those enclosed in a skin e.g. kidneys and chicken livers. Items that are enclosed in a skin or shell will burst, so you cannot cook eggs in their shells.

Small items and those not thicker than 5 cm (2'') will cook the most evenly, so arrange food in an even layer.

It is better to cook consecutive small batches rather than one large amount all at once.

Microwaves reduce the cooking time by about 75 %, so count the seconds rather than the minutes.

In microwave cooking less fat is absorbed so the quantities of fat can be reduced, which is ideal for people on a diet.

Never overcook — extra time can always be allowed, and remember that the heat built up within the food causes the food to continue cooking even after the oven is switched off.

Allow a short standing time for the heat to equalise.

Some foods need more delicate cooking than others. In the microwave oven you have a choice of settings. Cook eggs and cheese on low power ↙ to prevent curdling or toughening, and take care when reheating dishes containing cream.

Cover foods which require faster cooking, and to prevent drying out.

Use cling film either pierced or vented at one corner, or a lid, or greaseproof paper depending on whether you are cooking a wet or dry mixture.

Microwaves cook most strongly around the outside edges of food. Foods which are « stirrable » such as sauces and casseroles should be stirred during cooking.

Non-stirrable foods such as quiches, pies and joints of meat should be turned at regular intervals three times during cooking.

Some foods are best cooked more slowly — rice puddings, casseroles and rich fruit cakes should be cooked on Low power ↙ (this is stated in the recipes).

You must pay the same attention to your microwave cooking as you do when cooking in a saucepan, and it is perfectly alright to open the door to inspect the food. No heat loss will occur as no heat is produced by microwaves.

Browning

Microwaves do not brown although some browning will occur naturally in certain foods — e.g. a joint of beef will acquire a deeper hue.

You can first brown the meat in the traditional way (in a frying pan, under the grill or in the oven) and then continue cooking by microwave. Alternatively you can use the browning dish which has been specially designed for microwave cooking. This dish has a metaloxide base which reacts to the microwaves. The empty dish is heated in the microwave oven on Full Power ↙ for a few minutes (times are printed in the instruction leaflet). After this time the base of the dish becomes as hot as a frying pan and food to be browned should be added immediately. Since the dish retains its heat for a relatively short time, the food must either be previously brushed with oil or added immediately after oil (or butter) is put into the pre-heated dish. Press the meat flat on to the hot dish for maximum browning.

When the first side is browned, turn the piece over and brown the other side. If there is a large quantity of food to be browned on both sides, take the pieces out of the dish after one side is browned, wipe out the dish and replace it in the microwave oven for 2 to 3 minutes, when the dish will be sufficiently hot to brown the other side of the food.

The browning dish can also be used for « frying » eggs in a teaspoon of butter or oil. After browning the underside, prick the yolk and continue cooking in the microwave oven for 10 to 15 seconds.

If your browning dish has a cover, you can use ingredients such as vegetables and stock after the meat is seared by placing the lid on the top and continuing with casserole cooking.

Use chicken pieces, fillets of fish, sliced vegetables, chopped fruit.

Cover the food to retain the moisture, to avoid drying out and to prevent the food from spitting. Use the lid of the dish if it has one, or cling film, greaseproof paper or an upturned plate.

The browning dish browns the food. Pre-heat the browning dish as the metaloxide base of the dish collects heat in the same way as a grill. Food must be browned immediately the dish has been pre-heated as it does not keep its heat for very long.

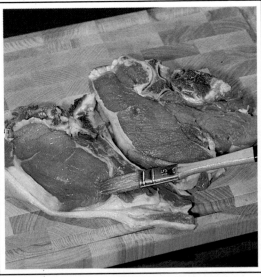

To brown meat you add either a mixture of butter and oil or oil the food beforehand. Brown it straightaway in the pre-heated dish. The latter solution takes away some of the heat collected in the dish.

Once the dish has been pre-heated, press the meat flat onto the hot surface for maximum browning.

When the first side is browned, turn the pieces over and brown the other side. If there is a large quantity to brown reheat the dish for 2 — 3 mins before browning the second side. This is the same for all types of food.

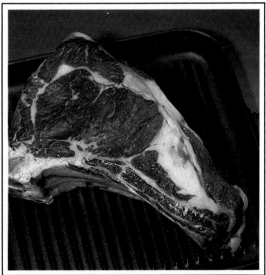

As a general rule, always stir or turn the food during cooking.
If you do not have a browning dish you can brown the meat in the traditional way (frying pan, grill, oven) after cooking in the microwave oven.

If you are preparing a side of beef (or chicken) for the grill or barbecue, start cooking on the barbecue and finish off in the microwave oven. (This can be reversed).

Reheating

Food reheated by microwaves does not spoil, lose its original flavour, dry out or change consistency, but remains as it was when first cooked, even potatoes, a nearly impossible task when reheated by traditional methods.

In a few minutes, sometimes in seconds, you can reheat a drink in a cup, a snack, a cooked dish or the contents of a can. Yesterday's meal will taste the same as yesterday when it was fresh.

It will only take 4 to 5 minutes to reheat 500 g (1 lb) of yesterday's left-overs or a meal that you had prepared earlier in the day. Reheat in a covered dish and stir during reheating, then leave to stand for a minute or two before serving.

If you are in doubt, choose the minimum cooking time and then add extra time afterwards if necessary. Allow the food to stand before serving.

Reheating in a microwave can simplify your life. You prepare the meals in advance and reheat them just before your meal time. Having organised your menus in advance, you will save precious time when you need it most. When reheating you will usually use Full Power ⏛, except for delicate dishes (those containing eggs or cream) or dishes which have a mixture of different ingredients, for example stews and dumplings. You may find it best to use the defrost programme ⚓ for some dishes.

Most dishes should be covered and the contents stirred during reheating and you will obtain even better results if you also turn the dish at equal intervals.

Rice presents no problem in reheating. It will not stick, nor does it change its flavour. For two portions allow 2 to 3 minutes on Full Power ⏛. Reheat the rice in a covered dish and stir once during reheating. Allow approximately the same amount of time for pasta.

A cup of tea, coffee or chocolate can be reheated in one minute on Full Power ⏛.

As with cooking, reheating times will vary according to the quantity, density and water content of the food. For example the contents of a 850 g (1 3/4 lb) can of peas will take about 5 minutes on Full Power but the contents of a can of runner beans will only take 2 minutes.

There is nothing better than a microwave to soften hard butter or chocolate to make a dessert.

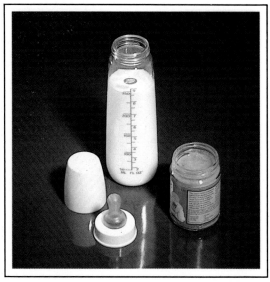

In seconds dry aromatic herbs or put back the freshness into stale cakes.

Feeding bottles must be prepared often. The microwaves let you heat up water in barely 1 minute ; a little pot will need about 1 1/2 mins (remember to remove the metal lid and replace it with cling film).
Older children will be able to reheat food without supervision and without running the risk of burning themselves.

Defrosting

With a microwave oven you can have a meal in minutes, whether it has been freshly cooked or thawed from its frozen state. Because of the speed of defrosting, there is less chance of deterioration or multiplication of bacteria which can occur if food is left standing at room temperature for several hours.

Good defrosting presupposes correct freezing, i.e. without large ice crystals. Ice crystals form a screen to the microwaves, slowing up the heating process. Ice-free food pieces will reheat quicker and in their turn melt the surrounding ice.

The pulsing of the defrost control causes the microwave energy to work intermittently ensuring more uniform defrosting throughout. This procedure is particularly important when defrosting fish and meat as otherwise the outside edges can begin to cook before the middle is thawed.

NEVER refreeze defrosted food.

Remember to remove frozen foods from any foil container and transfer to a suitable container (see section on containers).

Dishes which cannot be stirred should be thawed entirely on the defrost programme to ensure that the centre is fully thawed.

Microwaves are ideal for defrosting flaky or puff pastry. Allow 4 to 5 minutes for a block of about 400 g (14 oz) and thaw on the Defrost programme ⌣. Do not overthaw but roll as soon as the pastry is manageable.

Place the pastry in the dish and prick the base and sides with a fork which will ensure that the pastry does not rise too much during cooking. The pastry should be cool but not soft to the touch before cooking.

Thaw soft fruits uncovered on the Defrost setting 🖤. Shake the container from time to time or stir gently making sure that you do not break up the fruit.

Cooked dishes which are stirrable may be defrosted and reheated on Full Power 🖤. Allow 10 to 12 minutes for two portions i.e. 450 g (1 lb).

Bread defrosts very well in the microwave oven. Put the loaf on a paper serviette or piece of kitchen towel to absorb any excess moisture.

To obtain a good result, choose the defrost power. Reheating will then be even and the bread appetising.

A whole chicken takes about 22 mins to thaw on the defrost programme ⚓. It takes several hours to defrost a chicken by leaving it in the refrigerator (less if left at room temperature although this is not recommended from the point of view of hygiene).

To defrost large joints or whole poultry, put the joint in a dish so that no juices will seep onto the oven base, and turn the joint over halfway through the defrosting period. After allowing a short standing time, continue cooking. It is not recommended that you leave meat or poultry at room temperature in between the two operations.

When meat is defrosted by microwaves very little of the juices are lost. Leave the meat to stand for about 10 minutes before continuing cooking. Well defrosted meat will cook more evenly without drying out or excessive shrinkage.

If defrosted well, the meat will cook well and evenly without drying out. Season with salt and pepper after cooking and allow to stand before serving.

Defrosting

FISH/SHELLFISH	Quantity	Power	Times	Notes
Trout	250g/9oz	☃	3 mins.30 secs	Turn 1/2 way through defrosting.
Cod fillets	400g/14oz	☃	10-11 mins	Separate the fillets a.s.a.p. Let stand
Pieces of fish	100g/4oz	☃	3 mins	Separate the fillets a.s.a.p. Let stand
Prawns	200g/7oz	☃	2 to 3 mins	Shake the plate.

MEAT

Beef

Roast	1kg/2lb3oz	☃	25 to 30 mins	Turn 1/2 way through defrosting. Let stand.
Steaks	4 x 100g/4oz	☃	10 mins	Allow to stand after defrosting.
Pieces of meat	600g/1lb4oz	☃	8 to 10 mins	Allow to stand.
Minced steak	2 x 100g/4oz	☃	4 to 5 mins	Allow to stand.

Veal · Pork

Sides	450g/1lb	☃	8-10 mins	Allow to stand.
Roast	800g/1lb12oz	☃	25 mins	Allow to stand.

Lamb

Leg	1,5kg/3lb5oz	☃	30-35 mins	Allow to stand after defrosting.

Poultry

Whole chicken	800g/1lb12oz	☃	20-22 mins	Turn 1/2 way through defrosting. Allow to stand.
Legs	500g/1lb2oz	☃	5-6 mins	

FRUITS				
Strawberries	500g/1lb2oz	☃	8 mins	Shake the dish.
Raspberries	300g/11oz	☃	4 mins	Shake the dish.

Defrosting - Cooking

VEGETABLES				
Carrots	450g/1lb	♨	12-14 mins	In a covered dish.
Cauliflower	400g/14oz	♨	10-12 mins	In a covered dish.
Spinach	450g/1lb	♨	10-12 mins	In a covered dish.
Green beans	500g/1lb2oz	♨	12 mins	Shake covered dish.
Mixed vegetables	450g/1lb	♨	10-12 mins	Shake the dish
Peas	450g/1lb	♨	8-10 mins	Shake the dish

Reheating frozen dishes

COOKED DISHES				
Meat/fish	500g/1lb2oz	♨	12 mins	Put food in a covered Pyrex dish. Stir during cooking.
Quiche	4 individuals	♨	5 mins	Place in heated browning dish to avoid softening of the pastry.
Pizza	22cm/8 1/2'' diam.	♨	4 mins	Place in heated browning dish to avoid softening of the pastry.

DEFROSTING PROGRAMME				
Buns	4	☃	4 1/2 mins	On a paper serviette.
Croissants	4	☃	4 mins	On a paper serviette.

The times shown in the table below are examples. They will depend on the quality, amount and presentation of the food.

Breakfasts

Porridge

SERVES 4

100g/4oz porridge oats
2.5ml/1/2tsp salt
275ml/1/2 pint milk
150ml/1/4 pint water

METHOD

1. Combine all ingredients together in a bowl, stir well and cover with cling film.
2. Cook for 3-4 minutes on power ⏻, until the mixture boils. Stir 2 or 3 times during cooking.
3. Stand for 5 minutes and serve with milk and sugar to taste.

Sausage, bacon & egg

SERVES 1

10ml/2tsp butter
2 × 50g/2oz sausages, well pricked
1 rasher back bacon, rind removed
1 size 3 egg

METHOD

1. Pre-heat browning dish for 5 minutes on power ⏻.
2. Add the butter and sausages, turning the sausages to brown sides.
3. Cook for 2 minutes on power ⏻, then add the bacon and cook for a further minute.
4. Break the egg into the dish and cook for 1 minute on power ⏻.
5. Leave to stand for 2 minutes then serve.

Bacon, egg & tomato

SERVES 1

2 rashers back bacon, rind removed
1 medium tomato, halved
1 size 3 egg

METHOD

1. Put the bacon on a plate and cook for 30 seconds on power ⏻.
2. Place the tomato halves on the plate, cut side up.
3. Break the egg into a greased cup, puncture the yolk with a sharp knife, cover loosely with cling film and put on the plate with the bacon and tomato.
4. Cook for 1 1/2 minutes on power ⏻, turning the plate every 15 seconds.
5. Leave to stand for 30 seconds and then slide the egg out of the cup onto the plate.

Scrambled eggs

SERVES 1

2 size 3 eggs
30ml/2 tbsp milk
salt & pepper
10ml/2 tsp butter

METHOD

1. Lightly beat the eggs, milk, salt and pepper to taste, together in a small bowl.
2. Add the butter and cook for 1 1/2 to 2 minutes on power ⏻ until almost set. Stir twice during cooking.
3. Leave to stand for 1 minute before serving.

Soups

There is nothing better than a good soup to warm you up during winter.
And what would you say to an iced soup as a starter for a summer evening meal ? With micro-waves there is no need to plan a long time in advance. Just a few vegetables, a little butter and water... and a hearty soup is ready in about 10 minutes.

Both summer and winter vegetables cook well in a microwave.

To vary menus or to add to a finished meal, do not hesitate to add several cubes of ham, meat or fish... a winter vegetable soup with added cubes of duck conserve and, in a twinkling of an eye you have a festival soup.

So that the ingredients keep their flavour well, cook them in a little butter and only add very hot water at the end of cooking. Add the necessary egg or cream just before serving. If necessary reheat the dish for several seconds.

If you wish to prepare a soup in advance there is no problem. It will reheat perfectly without losing its colour or flavour.

For those in a great hurry you can use tinned or packet soup. Cover and stir half way through cooking.

Leek and potato soup

SERVES 4

450g/1lb leeks, washed, chopped
2 potatoes, peeled, diced
275ml/1/2 pint chicken stock
425ml/15fl oz milk
salt & pepper

METHOD

1. Place the prepared vegetables into a roaster bag. Tie loosely with an elastic band. Cook in the microwave for 10 minutes on power ⌣. Remove.

2. Heat the milk in a glass bowl for 3 minutes on power ⌣. Add the leeks and potatoes to the milk, and pour over stock. Season well.

3. Cook for 3 minutes on power ⌣. Cool slightly then liquidize.

Celery soup

SERVES 4

1 stick celery, washed, leaves
removed
15g/1/2 oz butter
225ml/8fl oz water
100ml/3 1/2fl oz fresh cream
225ml/8fl oz milk
chopped parsley to garnish

METHOD

1. Thinly slice the celery sticks and place in a casserole dish with the butter, salt and pepper and water. Cook covered for 10 minutes on power ☁.

2. Liquidize the mixture and add the milk and cream.

3. Reheat for 1 minute on power ☁, season and serve hot or cold garnished with the parsley.

Onion and potato soup

SERVES 4

200g/7oz potatoes, peeled, diced
200g/7oz onions, peeled, sliced
25g/1oz butter
100ml/3 1/2fl oz water
200ml/7fl oz milk
225/8fl oz boiling water
salt & pepper
chopped parsley to garnish

METHOD

1. Put the potatoes and onions in a large glass bowl and add the butter and water. Cover and cook for 8 minutes on power ♨, stirring occasionally.

2. Add the milk and boiling water and season with salt and pepper. Cook for a further 4 minutes on power ♨.

3. Check the seasoning and garnish with chopped parsley.

Variant : You can put this soup in the liquidizer and replace half the milk with cream.

French onion soup

SERVES 4

50g/2oz butter
450g/1lb sliced onions
30ml/2tbsp cornflour
850ml/1 1/2 pints water
salt & pepper
pinch cayenne pepper
2 beef stock cubes

METHOD

1. Melt butter in a large bowl on power ♨ for 1 minute.

2. Add the onions and stir. Cook for 5 minutes on power ♨, stirring twice.

3. Gradually stir in cornflour and crumbled stock cube and water. Add seasoning.

4. Cover with cling film and pierce the top.

5. Cook for 5 minutes on power ♨, stir well.

6. Serve with croutons or french toast and grated cheese.

7. Place a slice of toast plus cheese into each bowl and pop bowls individually into oven for 1 minute to melt cheese.

Chicken soup

SERVES 4

25g/1oz butter
1 medium onion, skinned and chopped
2 carrots, chopped
1 stick celery, chopped
30ml/2 tbsp cornflour
850ml/1 1/2 pints chicken stock
150ml/ 1/4 pint milk
salt & pepper
100g/4oz cooked chicken, cubed
30ml/2tbsp double cream

METHOD

1. Place butter into large bowl and melt for 1 minute on power ⌣.
2. Add onion, carrots and celery and cook for a further 1 1/2 minutes on power ⌣.
3. Blend cornflour with a little stock and add to vegetables with remaining stock.
4. Return to oven on power ⌣ for 5 minutes.
5. Remove from oven and liquidize until smooth.
6. Return to bowl and add milk, seasoning and chicken.
7. Cook for 10 minutes on power ⌣.
8. Stir in the cream just before serving.

Tomato soup

SERVES 4

15ml/1tbsp vegetable oil
100g/4oz chopped onions
450g/1lb tomatoes, peeled and sliced
15ml/1 tbsp tomato purée
15ml/1 tbsp Worcestershire sauce
salt & pepper
pinch paprika
2 beef stock cubes dissolved in
700ml/1 1/4 pints water
15ml/1 tbsp cornflour

METHOD

1. Pre-heat browning dish for 4 minutes on power ⌣ during last minute add oil.
2. Add onions and cook uncovered for 1 1/2 minutes on power ⌣.
3. Remove onions from dish and transfer to a suitable large bowl.
4. Add tomatoes, tomato purée, Worcestershire sauce, seasoning and stock, having first mixed the stock with cornflour. Stir well.
5. Cover with cling film and pierce the top.
6. Cook for 15 minutes on power ⌣, stirring every 5 minutes.

Cream of mushroom soup

SERVES 4

25g/1oz butter
15ml/1 tbsp cornflour
3 chicken stock cubes
600ml/1 pint hot water
300ml/ 1/2 pint milk
100g/4oz button mushrooms, sliced
salt & pepper
150ml/ 1/4 pint single cream
15ml/1 tbsp lemon juice
15ml/1 tbsp chopped parsley

METHOD

1. Place all ingredients barring cream, lemon juice and parsley into large bowl.
2. Cook uncovered for 5 minutes on power ⌣.
3. Lower heat to power ⌣ and cook for 12 minutes, stirring every 5 minutes.
4. Sieve or blend soup and cook for 4 minutes on power ⌣, add cream and heat for a further minute.
5. Add lemon juice and parsley before serving.

Salads, hors-d'œuvres, starters

Scallops, cooked fish, crispy bacon, liver pâté, prawns sautéed in oil all make a simple salad very appetising.

Serve the vegetables a little crisp with a herb vinaigrette dressing or a white cheese sauce.

A rabbit terrine, liver pâté, pork pâté will need approximately 10-20 minutes, less still if you prepare them in individual ramekins.

Liver pâté

SERVES 4

1 onion, peeled and chopped
50g/2oz butter
100g/4oz chicken livers, chopped
100g/4oz smoked ham, chopped
5ml/1 tsp mixed herbs
15ml/1 tbsp brandy
30ml/2tbsp double cream
salt & pepper
bay leaf

METHOD

1. Place the onion and half the butter in a shallow dish and cook for 3 minutes on power ⬚.

2. Stir in the chicken livers, ham and mixed herbs and cover with greaseproof paper. Cook for 5-7 minutes on power ⬚, stiring twice until the meat is cooked.

3. Blend until smooth.

4. Stir in brandy, cream and seasoning.

5. Spoon into serving dish and top with bay leaf.

6. Melt remaining butter in a bowl for 45 seconds on power ⬚, then pour over pâté. Chill in the refrigerator until butter hardens.

Vegetable terrine

SERVES 4

250g/9oz whole green beans, washed
250g/9oz carrots, peeled
100ml/3 1/2fl oz water
salt & pepper
200g/7oz cooked ham
3 size 3 eggs
30ml/2tbsp oil

METHOD

1. Cut the green beans and carrots into even sized strips.

2. Put the vegetables, water and salt and pepper into a glass dish. Cover and cook for 10 minutes on power ⬛.

3. Purée the ham in a food processor and add the eggs, oil and salt and pepper. Mix well.

4. Line the inside of a cake mould with greased greaseproof paper. Layer the inside of the mould by successively putting one layer of ham mousse, one layer of carrots, one layer of beans and so on. Finish with a layer of ham mousse.

5. Cook for 6 minutes on power ⬛.

6. Serve cold with a herb cheese or tomato purée.

Leek and bacon salad

SERVES 4

100g/4oz smoked bacon, rind removed
8 small leeks, washed, sliced
45ml/3 tbsp oil
15ml/1 tbsp vinegar
salt & pepper
pinch cayenne pepper

METHOD

1. Cut the bacon into small strips. Put the bacon and leeks into a glass dish, cover and cook for 10 minutes on power ⬛. Stir twice during cooking.

2. Whilst cooking, make a vinaigrette dressing by mixing all the remaining ingredients together.

3. Pour over the hot vegetables.

4. Serve this salad warm decorated with bay leaves.

Eggs and cheese

Cooking eggs in a microwave needs several precautions.

Do not try to cook an egg in its shell, as it will explode. .

Eggs consist of 2 substances, the white which is a protein, and the yolk which is a mixture of fatty globules, mineral elements, vitamins, etc.

Between the membrane, which surrounds the white and the yolk, and the shell there is air. When heated up this air puts pressure on the shell causing the egg to explode.

For fried eggs it is better to cook in 2 stages :
Start cooking by using only the white, then when it starts to become opaque add the yolk and heat for several seconds.

It will be difficult to make a soufflé in a microwave. The whites beaten into a « snow » will rise very quickly, only to sink as soon as taken out of the oven. In this case, it would be better to use whole eggs, beaten by hand (the whisk incorporates too much air) and to do the cooking using the defrosting programme.

There is no problem in cooking scrambled, or poached eggs. Cover whilst cooking.

As a general rule, remove eggs from the microwave before the desired cooking time is reached as they continue to cook a little by conduction.

Savoury cheese cake

SERVES 4

450ml/16fl oz warm milk
6 size 3 eggs
150g/5oz gruyère cheese, grated
pinch grated nutmeg
salt & pepper
15g/1/2oz butter

METHOD

1. Heat the milk for 2 minutes on power ⌣.

2. Beat the eggs in a bowl with the cheese, nutmeg, salt and pepper and milk.

3. Pour this mixture into a buttered glass dish.

4. Cook for 10 minutes on defrost setting ⌣ and then for a further 10 minutes on power ⌣.

5. Serve immediately.

Shellfish

Microwave cooking is measured in minutes, sometimes in seconds. This applies particularly to shellfish.

Several seconds too long and scallops will become rubbery and even explode. Overcooking will dry out shellfish.

Calculate the most precise cooking time and remember that the food will continue to cook for a short time after being removed from the oven.

When the recipe requires cooking of scallops, do so in small quantitites. Always cover them.

	Quantity	Power	Cooking Time	Notes
Prawns	200g/7oz	ᵐ	2 mins 30 secs	Cook them in a covered bowl without water.
Scampi	500g/18oz	ᵐ	4 1/2 mins/ 5 mins	Cook them in a covered bowl without water. Turn the dish during cooking.
Mussels	500g/18oz	ᵐ	4 mins	Cook in a covered glass dish with butter, shallots and white wine. Stir several times during cooking.
Scallops	8	ᵐ	2 1/2-3 mins	Cook in a covered glass dish with a little butter. Turn 1/2 way through cooking. Allow to stand.

Sweet and sour prawns

SERVES 4

12 large prawns
30ml/2tbsp oil
clove garlic, peeled, crushed
5ml/1tsp ground ginger
60ml/4tbsp Worcestershire sauce
15ml/1tbsp granulated sugar
60ml/4tbsp tomato ketchup
salt & pepper
4 tomatoes, sliced

METHOD

1. Wash and dry the prawns.

2. Pre-heat a browning dish for 4 minutes on power ᵐ.

3. Add the oil and sauté the prawns in the browning dish. Cover and cook the prawns for 4 minutes on power ᵐ, stirring frequently.

4. Set the prawns aside with the juices.

5. Reheat the browning dish for 1 minute on power ᵐ, and add the crushed garlic, ginger, Worcestershire sauce, sugar, ketchup and salt and pepper.

6. Cook for 1 minute on power ᵐ and serve with the prawns and fresh tomatoes.

Scallops

SERVES 4

350g/12oz button mushrooms, sliced
75g/3oz butter
juice of half a lemon
15ml/1tbsp oil
8 scallops
30ml/2tbsp white Vermouth
salt & pepper
30ml/2tbsp chives finely chopped

METHOD

1. Put the mushrooms and 15 g/1/2oz of butter and lemon juice into a glass bowl and cook for 5 minutes on power ⏣. Put to one side.

2. Preheat a browning dish for 5 minutes on power ⏣.

3. Add 15g/1/2oz butter and oil to the browning dish. Add the scallops turning them and then the Vermouth and salt and pepper.

4. Cook for 1 minute on power ⏣.

5. Gradually add the remaining butter and mushrooms to the scallops and mix together well. Garnish with the chopped chives.

Paella

SERVES 4

30ml/2tbsp oil
2 chicken legs
1/2 red pepper, deseeded, chopped
1/2 green pepper, deseeded
chopped
1 onion, peeled, chopped
clove garlic, peeled, crushed
250g/9oz frozen peas
100g/4oz rice
pinch saffron powder
bouquet garni
salt & pepper
1/2 litre / 3/4pt mussels
8 small langoustines
45ml/3tbsp water
pinch salt
100 g/4oz peeled prawns

METHOD

1. Preheat a browning dish for 6 minutes on power ⬚. Add the oil and then brown the chicken on all sides.

2. Remove the chicken and reheat the browning dish for a further 3 minutes on power ⬚.

3. Add the peppers, onion, garlic and peas, stirring well. Then add the rice, saffron, bouquet garni and twice the volume of rice in water.

4. Cover the dish with cling film and cook for 10 minutes on power ⬚. Add the chicken and season with salt and pepper and cook for a further 7 minutes on power ⬚.

5. Put the mussels in a dish to open them and cook for 5 minutes on power ⬚. Set aside.

6. Place the langoustines in a dish with the water and salt. Cook for 3 minutes on power ⬚.

7. Add the langoustines, mussels and the prawns to the rest of the dish and heat for 3 minutes on power ⬚. Serve straightaway.

King prawns in sorrel

SERVES 4

2 medium sized courgettes, cut into
strips
15g/1/2oz butter
5ml/1tsp thyme
6 leaves sorrel, cut in thin strips
salt & pepper
200ml/7fl oz water
pinch curry powder
12 king prawns, peeled

METHOD

1. Put the courgettes in a dish with the butter and the thyme. Cover and cook for 5 minutes on power ⬚.

2. Add the sorrel to the courgettes with the salt and pepper and cook for a further minute on power ⬚. Set aside.

3. Put the water in a large bowl, season with pepper and add the curry powder, heat for 2 minutes on power ⬚.

4. Add the prawns and cook for a further 6 minutes on power ⬚. Strain the prawns.

5. Serve with the courgettes in sorrel.

Fish

It is fish that has made microwaves well known. This is not a whim as fish cooked well in a microwave stays tender, firm and keeps all its flavour. After several attempts, you will know how to cook it to the exact temperature required, and then your menus will often include seafood.

Choose fillets, steaks, or small even pieces of fish. These cook more evenly and children cannot complain about bones. Choose very fresh fish as microwaves bring out the flavours, even bad ones.

You can cook fish in a dish, alone, or in buttered greaseproof paper without fat, with herbs or vegetables — then dieting becomes a pleasure. If you wish to prepare roast fish, make sure you have a browning dish — the results are excellent.
Another advantage of a microwave is the absence of fishy cooking smells.

Always let fish stand for several minutes before serving. As with other food, fish continues to cook for a little while after having been removed from the oven.

Finally, microwaves allow you to serve perch or bream on the barbecue, grilled but not burnt. All you need to do is to grill the fish on the surface on the barbecue, then finish the cooking in a microwave oven. Thus no burnt fish on the outside and well cooked inside.

The times shown in the following tables and recipes are examples. They will vary depending on the quality, freshness, size, thickness etc. of the fish and, of course, on your own taste.

FISH	Quantity	Power	Cooking time	Notes
Brill or turbot	4 fillets	♨	4 mins	Cook covered on their own or with 15g/1/2oz butter, 1 shallot and 15ml/1tbsp white wine. Check cooking according to the thickness of the fillets. Allow to stand.
Cod	2 steaks 400g/14oz	♨	1st side, 2 mins 2nd side, 2 1/2 mins	Cook in a covered dish with 15g/1/2oz butter (1 shallot and 15ml/1tbsp white wine - optional). Turn the dish during cooking.
Bream	600g/1lb 6oz	♨	1st side, 3 mins 2nd side, 2 1/2 mins	Cook in a covered dish with 15g/1/2oz butter (1 shallot and 15ml/1tbsp white wine - optional). Turn the dish during cooking. Allow to stand.

FISH	Quantity	Power	Cooking time	Notes
Turbot	300g/11oz 2 steaks/ fillets		1st side, 2 mins 2nd side, 1 1/2 mins	Stew 1 grated shallot in 15 g/1/2oz butter in a covered glass dish, add 15ml/1tbsp white wine and seasoned fish. Turn the dish during cooking. Allow to stand.
Mackeral	2-225g/8oz		4 to 5 mins	Cook on their own or in a small quantity of wine stock. Turn the dish during cooking. Allow to stand.
Whiting	2 fillets 250g/9oz		1st side, 1 1/2 mins 2nd side, 45 secs	Cook in a covered dish with 15g/1/2oz butter, (1 shallot and 15ml/1 tbsp white wine - optional). Turn the dish during cooking. Allow to stand
Whiting	200g/7oz		1st side, 2 mins 2nd side, 2 1/2 mins	Flour the fish lightly. Cook in a browning dish. (preheated for 4 mins) with 15ml/ 1tbsp oil and 15g/1/2oz butter. Allow to stand.
Skate	300g/11oz		1st side, 1 min 45 secs 2nd side, 3 1/2 mins	Cook in a covered dish with 1 grated shallot, 30ml/2tbsp water, dash of vinegar, salt and pepper. Turn the dish during cooking. Allow to stand.
Red mullet	250g/9oz		1st side, 1 min 2nd side, 1 1/4 mins	Braise with butter, shallot and white wine in a covered dish. Allow to stand.
Whole red Mullet	200g/7oz		1st side, 2 mins 2nd side, 3 mins	Cook with olive oil in a browning dish preheated for 3 mins. Cover. Allow to stand.
John Dory	600g/ 1lb 6oz		1st side, 2 mins 2nd side, 1 1/2 mins	Preheat the browning dish for 4 mins. Cook with skin in a mixture of oil and butter. Turn the dish during cooking. Allow to stand.
Salmon	2 steaks 300g/11oz		1st side, 2 mins 2nd side, 1 min	Stew 1 grated shallot in 15g/1/2oz butter, add 15ml/1 tbsp white wine and the fish. Allow to stand.
Sole	2 small ones		1st side, 2 mins 2nd side, 1 1/2 mins	Lightly flour the soles. Preheat the browning dish for 5 mins. Add 15g/1/2oz butter and 15ml/1 tbsp oil and brown the soles. Return after 2 mins. Allow to stand.
Sole	2 small ones		1st side, 2 mins 2nd side, 2 mins	Cook the soles (without skins) in a glass dish without adding anything. Serve with a dash of lemon and a knob of butter.
Trout	400g/14oz		4 mins	Cook in a covered dish with a little butter. Turn the dish during cooking. Allow to stand.

Fillet of cod with wine and cream

SERVES 4

3 shallots, peeled and chopped
6 button mushrooms, washed
sliced
juice of half a lemon
salt & pepper
4 cod fillets, fresh or frozen (about
450g/1lb)
150ml/ 1/4 pint white wine
30ml/2tbsp cream

METHOD

1. Place shallots and mushrooms in the bottom of an ovenproof casserole dish. Add lemon juice, salt and pepper.

2. Place cod fillets on top, season and pour over wine. Cover dish with
cling film and cook for 6 minutes on power ☙, turning dish once
during cooking.

3. Place the fish onto a plate and set to one side. Add the cream to
the stock in the casserole dish and cook without covering for
4 minutes on power ☙ to thicken, stirring frequently.

4. Add fish fillets to sauce and reheat for 1 1/2 minutes on power ☙.

Mackeral in white sauce

SERVES 4

4 mackeral, cleaned, and gutted
1 carrot, peeled, sliced
1 onion, peeled, sliced
1/2 lemon, cut in half
5ml/1tsp thyme
15g/1/2oz butter
salt & pepper
200ml/7fl oz dry white wine

METHOD

1. Arrange the mackeral in a large casserole dish, add the carrot, onion,
lemon pieces, thyme and butter.

2. Season with salt and pepper and pour over the white wine.

3. Cover dish and cook for 7 minutes on power ☙, turning the fish over
1/2 way through cooking. Allow to cool.

Cod in parsley sauce

SERVES 4

4 cod steaks
300ml/1/2 pint parsley sauce

METHOD

1. Place cod steaks in a shallow dish and cover with greaseproof paper.
2. Cook for 4-5 minutes on power ⏻.
3. Remove greaseproof paper and pour over prepared parsley sauce.
4. Cook for 30 seconds on power ⏻.

Trout with almonds

SERVES 4

2 trout, cleaned and gutted
30ml/2tbsp flour
50g/2oz butter
25g/1oz flaked almonds
salt & pepper

METHOD

1. Pre-heat the browning dish for 5 minutes on power ⌣.

2. Coat the trout in the flour.

3. Put the trout and 25g/1oz butter in the browning dish and turn the trout to brown all over.

4. Without covering, cook the trout for 2 minutes on power ⌣.

5. Add remaining butter and almonds and turn the trout over.

6. Cook for 1 minute on power ⌣, and season.

Skate in spicy tomato sauce

SERVES 4

30ml/2tbsp oil
1 onion, peeled, chopped
clove of garlic, peeled, crushed
425g/15oz tin tomatoes, strained
salt & pepper
4 drops tabasco sauce
15ml/1tbsp capers
30ml/2tbsp parsley, chopped
800g/1 3/4lbs skate
30ml/2tbsp vinegar
30ml/2tbsp water
1 shallot, peeled, sliced

METHOD

1. Pour the oil into a casserole dish, add the onion and garlic. Cover and cook for 1 1/2 minutes on power ⌣.

2. Add the tomatoes and salt and pepper. Cover and cook for 4 minutes on power ⌣. Then add the capers and parsley and cook for a further minute on power ⌣. Set aside.

3. Cook the skate in a dish with the vinegar, water and shallot, covered for 3 1/2 minutes on each side on power ⌣.

4. Remove the skin and fish bones and flake the flesh in the sauce. Serve with rice or pasta.

Plaice in carrots and white wine butter

SERVES 4

400g/14oz carrots, peeled, cut into fine strips
1 shallot, peeled, sliced
25g/1oz butter
30ml/2tbsp water
4 plaice fillets
salt & pepper

White wine butter sauce :
1 shallot, peeled, chopped
125ml/4fl oz white wine
salt & pepper
75g/3oz butter

METHOD

1. Put the carrots, shallot, butter and water into a large casserole dish. Cover, and cook for 8 minutes on power ⌣.

2. Arrange the plaice fillets on the carrots and season with salt and pepper. Cover and cook for 2 minutes on each side on power ⌣. Set aside.

3. Put the finely chopped shallot, white wine and salt and pepper in a small dish. Boil on power ⌣ until only 45ml/3tabl of liquid remains.

4. Add the butter cut into cubes and heat for 30 seconds on power ⌣, whisk.

5. Put one fillet of fish on each plate with 1/4 of the carrots and pour the sauce over the fish.

Plaice in cucumber and coriander sauce

SERVES 4

1 cucumber
25g/1oz butter
1 shallot, peeled, sliced
juice of a lemon
salt & pepper
125ml/4fl oz fresh cream
600g/1 1/4lbs plaice fillets
2.5ml/1/2tsp coriander grains
15ml/1tbsp fresh chervil, chopped

METHOD

1. Peel the cucumber and cut into 4 lengthwise, remove the seeds and cut the flesh into slices.

2. Put the cucumber slices and half the butter, shallot, juice of half the lemon and salt and pepper into a casserole dish. Cover and cook for 4 minutes on power ⌣.

3. Liquidize the mixture and add the cream. Reheat for 1 minute without covering on power ⌣.

4. Put the plaice fillets in a casserole dish and add the remaining butter, sprinkle the fish with coriander grains and add the remaining lemon juice, season. Cover and cook the fish for 2 minutes on each side on power ⌣.

5. Coat the fish in the cucumber sauce and sprinkle with chopped chervil. If necessary reheat for 30 seconds on power ⌣.

Plaice curry

SERVES 4

15ml/1tbsp oil
1 onion, peeled, chopped
5ml/1tsp curry powder
1 tomato, skinned, chopped
1 apple, peeled, cubed
15ml/1tbsp raisins
125 ml/4oz cream
salt & pepper
2 plaice fillets, skinned, rolled.

METHOD

1. Preheat the browning dish for 6 minutes on power ⌣.

2. Add the oil and onion and cook for 1 minute on power ⌣.
   Add the curry powder and cook for a further minute. Stir well.

3. Add tomato, apple, raisins, cream and salt and pepper stirring well.
   Cover dish and cook for 5 minutes on power ⌣.

4. Add the plaice fillets to the mixture and cook for 4 minutes on power
   ⌣. Serve with saffron rice.

Whiting in cress sauce

SERVES 4

1 bunch watercress, washed
50g/2oz butter
150ml/5fl oz fresh cream
salt & pepper
4 whiting fillets
1 shallot, peeled, sliced
30ml/2 tbsp white wine.

METHOD

1. Put the watercress and half of the butter into a casserole dish and cook for 3 minutes on power ⬚.

2. Liquidize the watercress and add the cream and salt and pepper. Pour back into the dish and cook for 2 minutes on power ⬚. Set aside.

3. Arrange the whiting fillets in a dish and add remaining butter, shallot and white wine. Cook for 4 1/2 minutes on power ⬚.

4. Pour the cooking juices from the fish into the sauce.
   Strain this through a sieve over the fish and serve immediately with boiled potatoes.

Whiting in mushroom sauce

SERVES 4

250g/9oz button mushrooms, sliced
1 shallot, peeled, chopped
125ml/4fl oz white wine
juice of half a lemon
25g/1oz butter
4 whiting fillets
salt & pepper
30ml/2 tbsp fresh cream
15ml/1 tbsp mixed herbs

METHOD

1. Put the mushrooms, shallot, white wine, lemon juice and butter into a large casserole dish. Cover and cook for 3 minutes on power ⬚. Set aside.

2. Pour the cooking juices from the mushrooms into a glass dish. Add the whiting fillets to the mushrooms and season with salt and pepper. Cover and cook for 2 minutes on power ⬚. Turn the fillets over and cook for a further 1 1/2 minutes.

3. Mix the reserved cooking juices with the fresh cream, add the mushrooms and coat the fillets of fish.

4. Garnish with finely chopped herbs.

Tuna bake

SERVES 4

100g/4oz peas
25g/1oz butter
200g/7oz tin tuna fish, drained
1 large tomato, sliced
175g/6oz cheddar cheese, grated
225 ml/8fl oz condensed mushroom
soup
salt & pepper
pinch paprika powder

METHOD

1. Put peas and butter into a suitable dish, cover with cling film and cook for 2 minutes on power ⏻.
2. Add the tuna fish, tomato and half the grated cheese to the peas.
3. Pour over mushroom soup and season with salt and pepper.
4. Cook for 4 minutes on power ⏻ turning the dish after 2 minutes.
5. Sprinkle on remaining cheese and paprika and return to oven for a further minute on power ⏻ to melt cheese.

Haddock with leeks and cheese

SERVES 4

600g/1 1/4lbs haddock
3 leeks, washed, cut into strips
25g/1oz butter
200g/7oz cream cheese
5ml/1tsp mustard powder
peel of half a lemon, chopped
15ml/1 tbsp chervil, chopped
salt & pepper

METHOD

1. Soak the haddock in water for 2 hours.

2. Put the leeks and butter into a casserole dish, cover and cook for 7 minutes on power ⌣. Stir well.

3. Add the haddock and cook for a further 3 minutes on power ⌣.

4. Prepare the sauce by mixing together the cream cheese, mustard, lemon peel, chervil and salt and pepper. Serve cold with the hot fish.

Fisherman's pot in basil

SERVES 4

2 carrots, peeled
1 small courgette, washed
100g/4oz french beans
75g/3oz butter
45ml/3 tbsp water
2 shallots, peeled, sliced
15ml/1 tbsp oil
30ml/2 tbsp dry white wine
4 scallops, shelled
4 small plaice fillets
175g/6oz prawns, peeled
salt & pepper
6 leaves basil, chopped

METHOD

1. Cut the vegetables into strips - removing the hard core of the carrots and the seeds from the courgettes. Cut the french beans in two.

2. Put 25g/1oz of butter, water, carrots and french beans in a glass casserole dish. Cover, and cook for 5 minutes on power ⌣.

3. Add the courgettes and cook for a further 3 minutes on power ⌣. Put aside.

4. In a glass dish, braise the finely sliced shallots in the oil for 1 minute on power ⌣. Add the white wine, scallops, plaice fillets, prawns and salt and pepper. Cook for 4 minutes on power ⌣, turning the dish during cooking.

5. Pour the cooking juices from the vegetables and fish into a small dish and add the remaining butter. Cook for 30 seconds on power ⌣ and whisk. Add the chopped basil.

6. Coat the fish and serve with the vegetables.

Fish terrine

SERVES 4

600g/1 1/4 lb whiting fillets (or another white fish)
3 size 3 eggs
125ml/4fl oz fresh cream
pinch powdered coriander
salt & pepper
1 smoked fish fillet

METHOD

1. Put the whiting fillets through the food processor with the eggs, cream and coriander, salt and pepper.

2. Remove the skin and the bones of the smoked fish.
Keep the fillets whole.

3. Grease a pyrex cake mould with butter and pour 1/2 of the whiting sauce into it. Then add the smoked fish fillets and cover with the rest of the sauce.

4. Cover the mould with a sheet of buttered greaseproof paper and cook for 5 mins on power ⌣. Remove the paper and cook for a further 3 minutes. Allow to stand for 5 minutes before removing from the mould.

a) Serve hot with a white wine and butter sauce or with melted butter and finely chopped herbs.

b) Serve cold with sliced artichokes, asparagus or courgettes and vinaigrette or with white herb cheese.

Fillet of plaice with parsley and chives

SERVES 2

2 plaice fillets
salt & pepper
5ml/1tsp lemon juice
10ml/2tsp oil
5ml/1tsp freshly chopped chives
5ml/1tsp freshly chopped parsley

METHOD

1. Put the plaice fillets in a shallow dish and season lightly.

2. Add lemon juice and oil, cover with cling film and cook for 3 minutes on power ⬚.

3. Uncover dish and sprinkle the chives and parsley over the fish.

Herrings in mustard sauce

SERVES 4

4 herrings
10ml/2tsp Dijon mustard
salt & pepper
100ml/3 1/2 fl oz water
5ml/1tsp vinegar
125ml/4fl oz fresh cream

METHOD

1. Paint the herrings with the mustard and season with salt and pepper. Arrange in a casserole dish and add the water and vinegar.

2. Cover and cook for 6 minutes, 3 minutes on each side on power ⬚. Set aside.

3. Pass the cooking juices through a sieve into a small casserole dish. Add the fresh cream and cook for 5 minutes on power ⬚.

4. Check the seasoning and coat the fish.

Poultry, rabbit

Poultry and rabbit cook very well in a microwave. They stay tender and juicy.

When cooking whole poultry — chicken, duck, guinea-fowl — you will save precious time over traditional cooking. Of course, the skin will not be crusty but it will still look appetising. In fact, every piece cooked for more than 20 minutes in a microwave will colour with the browning of the fats.

This delay does not occur if you have a browning dish.

Heat it empty for 6-7 minutes then put the lightly-oiled fowl in the dish. The skin will brown immediately. As duck is very greasy, remove excess grease 1/2 way through cooking.

You will save more time by cooking pieces of poultry. Put the thickest pieces around the outside of the dish, the thinner ones inside. Cover the dish and turn it during cooking.

Chicken or duck legs will need 1-2 minutes more than other pieces. Season at the end of cooking.

Allow the cooked food to stand whilst finishing the sauce or accompanying dish. For the cooking base 1/2 or even 1/4 of the liquid needed for traditional cooking will be sufficient. There is no time for the liquid to evaporate and poultry produces very little juice.

If you want to barbecue poultry, cook it partially in a microwave. This way you'll avoid burning the outside, but it will still be cooked inside. There is no problem for stuffed poultry. The times shown in the following recipes and tables are examples. The will vary according to quality, size, thickness and taste.

POULTRY/ RABBIT	Quantity	Power	Cooking time	Notes
Duckling	1 kg/ 21b3oz	⊔	16-18 mins Cook longer according to taste.	Pre-heat the browning dish for 5 mins. Cook the duckling lightly oiled. Separate the legs 1/2 way through cooking. Allow to stand for 10 minutes.
Guinea-Fowl	1 kg/ 2lb3oz	⊔	16-18 mins	Pre-heat the browning dish for 7 minutes. Cook the guinea fowl in a mixture of oil and butter. Separate the legs after 10 minutes to help cooking. Allow to stand for 5-10 minutes.
Chicken	1 kg/ 2lb3oz	⊔	20 mins	Lightly butter the chicken. Cook in a dish without covering. Separate the legs after 10 minutes and continue cooking. Allow to stand.
Chicken pieces	2 wings 2 legs	⊔	6 mins 8 mins	Preheat the browning dish for 6 minutes. Cook the pieces in a mixture of butter and oil. Turn the pieces.
Rabbit pieces	1,5kg/ 3lb5oz	⊔	12-14 mins	Preheat the browning dish for 6 minutes. Add 30ml/2tbsp oil and brown. Cook for 12 minutes. Cover after 5 minutes. Season when 1/2 cooked. Allow to stand.
Turkey legs	800 g/ 11b12oz	⊔	27 mins	Preheat the browning dish for 5 minutes. Cook the lightly oiled turkey uncovered. Turn the turkey dish during cooking.

Chicken and shallots

SERVES 4

50g/2oz butter
15ml/1 tbsp butter
1,2kg/2 3/4lb chicken, cut in 8 pieces
250g/9oz shallots, peeled
salt & pepper

METHOD

1. Preheat the browning dish for 6 minutes on power ⏻. Add 15g/1/2oz butter and oil to the browning dish. Brown the chicken on all sides. Set aside.

2. Reheat the browning dish for 3 minutes on power ⏻, then brown the shallots stirring with a wooden spoon.

3. When they are brown, add the chicken, cover and cook for 10 minutes on power ⏻. After 8 minutes season with salt and pepper. Turning the dish during cooking.

4. When the chicken is cooked, remove it from the browning dish with half the shallots. Put the other half in a liquidizer with the cooking juices.

5. Pour liquid back into the browning dish with the remaining butter. Stir well. Add the chicken and the whole shallots and heat for 30 seconds on power ⏻.

Roast chicken

SERVES 4

25g/1oz butter
5ml/1tsp paprika
1,4kg/3lb roasting chicken

METHOD

1. Melt butter in a small bowl for 45 seconds on power ⏚.
2. Add paprika and stir.
3. Brush the chicken liberally with the melted butter mix.
4. Place the chicken in a roasting bag, tie the end with string and pierce the bag to let steam escape.
5. Place in a dish breast side down and cook for 6 minutes on power ⏚.
6. Turn the chicken breast side up and cook for a further 12 minutes.
7. Remove chicken from roasting bag and cover with foil and allow to stand for 15 minutes before serving.

Chicken in cheese

SERVES 4

30ml/2tbsp oil
1,2kg/2 3/4lb chicken, cut into 8 pieces
15g/1/2oz butter
12 small onions, peeled
1 shallot, peeled, chopped
125g/5oz cheese (Emmenthal, Gruyère), cut into strips

METHOD

1. Preheat the browning dish for 5 minutes on power ⏚. Coat the chicken pieces in the oil and brown in the browning dish.
2. Add the butter, whole onions and shallots. Cover and cook for 8 minutes on power ⏚. Turn the meat during cooking.
3. Strain off the excess juice, then place the strips of cheese over the chicken. Season with salt and pepper and cook for 2 minutes on power ⏚.
4. Serve with a green salad.

Chicken and spices

SERVES 4

15ml/1tbsp black pepper
15ml/1tbsp aniseed or fennel grains
3 cloves garlic
5ml/1tsp salt
5ml/1tsp powdered ginger
30ml/2tbsp white Vermouth
1,2kg/21b12oz chicken

METHOD

1. Crush the pepper, aniseed, garlic, salt and ginger together. Add the vermouth and mix all the ingredients together in a liquidizer.

2. Coat the chicken with this mixture and also stuff the chicken with it.

3. Put the chicken into a glass casserole dish and cover. Cook for 15 minutes on power ⏚, turning the dish during cooking.

4. After 15 minutes remove the lid and cook the chicken for a further 5 minutes on power ⏚.

5. Serve straightaway with the cooking juices.

Chicken in lemon

SERVES 4

1 lemon, washed
1 chicken cut into 8 pieces
30ml/2tbsp oil
1 carrot, peeled, grated
1 small onion, peeled, grated
1 leek, white part only, grated
125ml/4fl oz chicken stock
salt & pepper
65g/2 1/2oz butter
30ml/2tbsp chopped chives

METHOD

1. Preheat a browning dish for 5 minutes on power ⏚.

2. Remove the rind from the lemon and cut into very fine strips. Plunge them into boiling water for 1 minute. Squeeze the lemon and retain the juice.

3. Lightly oil the chicken pieces and brown them in the browning dish for 3 minutes on power ⏚.

4. Add the vegetables, chicken stock, lemon rind and juice, salt and pepper. Cook, covered for 6 minutes on power ⏚.

5. Put the chicken aside and allow to stand. Pour the cooking juices into a bowl and heat for 1 1/2 minutes on power ⏚. Add the butter, heat for 30 seconds on power ⏚, then whisk.

6. Add the chopped chives, mix and coat the chicken in this sauce.

Chicken with aubergines

SERVES 4

90ml/6tbsp oil
1,2kg/2 3/4lb chicken, cut into 8 pieces
2 aubergines, washed, sliced
1 onion, peeled, sliced
2 cloves garlic, peeled, crushed
salt & pepper
6 leaves mint, finely chopped

METHOD

1. Preheat a browning dish for 6 minutes on power ⬳. Add 30ml/2tbsp oil and brown the chicken pieces on all sides. Remove.

2. Heat the browning dish again for 4 minutes on power ⬳. Add 30ml/2tbsp oil and brown the aubergines. Do this several times adding oil if necessary and reheating the dish. Drain the aubergines onto absorbent paper.

3. Add the onion and garlic to the dish with a little oil, then add the chicken and cover with layers of aubergine. Season with salt and pepper.

4. Cover the dish and cook for 10 minutes on power ⬳. Serve with the finely chopped mint.

Paprika chicken

SERVES 4

700g/1 1/2lb chicken pieces, skins
removed
25g/1oz flour
15ml/1tbsp paprika
1 green pepper, deseeded, chopped
100g/4oz button mushrooms, washed, sliced
300ml/ 1/2 pint chicken stock
small carton soured cream
salt & pepper

METHOD

1. Toss the chicken pieces in the flour and fry in a frying pan until
   brown.

2. Remove the chicken from the pan. Mix the paprika with a little water
   to form a thick paste. Spread this over the chicken.

3. Place the chicken, chopped peppers, mushrooms and stock into a
   casserole dish.

4. Cook for 12 minutes on power ⏚. Stirring once during this cycle.

5. Check the seasoning, just before serving pour on the soured cream.

Chicken in red wine

SERVES 4

30ml/2tbsp oil
1kg/2lb3oz chicken, cut into 8 pieces
bouquet garni
2 sticks celery, washed, chopped
225ml/8fl oz red wine
100g/4oz bacon, chopped
clove of garlic, chopped
salt & pepper
15g/1/2oz butter
5ml/1tsp parsley, chopped
5ml/1tsp chives, chopped

METHOD

1. Preheat a browning dish for 6 minutes on power ⏚.

2. Lightly oil the chicken pieces and put them into the browning dish
   turning them so that they brown on both sides.

3. Add the bouquet garni and the celery and cook covered, for 6 minutes on power ⏚.

4. Add the wine, bacon, garlic and salt and pepper. Mix well, cover and
   cook for 6 minutes on power ⏚.

5. Stir in the butter and garnish with the finely chopped herbs.

Duck in orange sauce

SERVES 4

1,4kg/3lb duck, washed
30ml/2tbsp oil
15ml/1 tbsp cornflour
grated rind and juice 1 orange
150ml/1/4 pint red wine
150ml/1/4 pint chicken stock
salt & pepper
15ml/1 tbsp sugar

METHOD

1. Place the duck skin side up on a roasting rack in a large shallow dish. Brush the skin lightly all over with the oil. Cover with grease-proof paper and cook for 12 minutes on power ⏻, turning the dish 3 times during cooking.

2. Turn the duck over and cook for a further 15 minutes on power ⏻, turning the dish during cooking. Place duck on a serving dish.

3. Place the cornflour and the orange rind in a bowl. Mix to a smooth paste with the orange juice, wine and stock. Season and add the sugar. Stir well.

4. Cook for 2 minutes on power ⏻, whisk and then cook for a further 1 minute on power ⏻.

5. Pour half the sauce over the duck and serve the remaining sauce separately.

Duck with vegetables

SERVES 4

50g/2oz butter
15ml/1tbsp oil
1 duck cut into pieces
5ml/1tsp dried thyme
8 small onions, peeled
300g/11oz carrots, peeled, cubed
200g/7oz turnips, peeled, cubed
salt & pepper

METHOD

1. Preheat a browning dish for 6 minutes on power ⏻. Add 15g/1/2oz butter and the oil and brown the pieces of duck on each side. Sprinkle duck with the dried thyme. Cover dish and cook for 5 minutes on power ⏻. Remove and set aside.

2. Add remaining butter to the browning dish and add the vegetables, stir well. Cover and cook for 5 minutes on power ⏻.

3. Add the duck, salt and pepper and cook for 5 minutes on power ⏻.

Chicken à la King

SERVES 4

50g/2oz butter
100g/4oz frozen peas
100g/4oz mushrooms, sliced
50g/2oz flour
300ml/1/2 pint milk
300ml/1/2 pint chicken stock
350g/12oz cooked chicken, diced
2.5ml/1/2tsp celery salt
pepper
15ml/1 tbsp single cream

METHOD

1. Put the butter in a bowl and melt for 45 seconds on power ⚨.
2. Add the peas and mushrooms and stir and cook for 2 minutes on power ⚨.
3. Stir in the flour and gradually add the milk and chicken stock, stirring all the time.
4. Cook for 4 minutes on power ⚨, stirring once during cooking.
5. Add the chicken pieces and cook for a further 2 minutes on power ⚨.
6. Season and stir in the single cream.
7. Serve on a bed of rice.

Rabbit casserole

SERVES 4

1kg/2 1/2lb boneless rabbit pieces
30ml/2 tbsp flour
salt & pepper
2 medium onions, peeled, chopped
2 large carrots, peeled, sliced
450ml/3/4 pint beef stock
5ml/1tsp mixed herbs

METHOD

1. Coat the rabbit pieces in the flour seasoned with salt and pepper.
2. Put the rabbit, onions, carrots, beef stock and mixed herbs into a 3 litre/6 pint casserole dish. Stir well and cover with cling film.
3. Cook for 30 minutes on power ⚨, stirring the casserole every 5 minutes. Season well.

Meat

Meat cooks well in a microwave oven. Pork and lamb give slightly better results than beef or veal.

Microwaves are not very suitable for stewing or boiling meat.

If you are cooking a joint, remember to turn the meat and the dish during cooking.

If you are cooking cubes of meat, remember to stir from time to time.

A browning dish is indispensable when cooking meat.

When roasting or sautéeing, remove any excess cooking juices after having browned one side.

It is not necessary to divide meat into pieces. In fact veal and roast beef are better whole than cut into pieces.

Only use half the quantity of liquid used in traditional cooking.

Do not forget to allow the meat to stand before serving and cover the dish during this time. The meat will remain hot.

Season after cooking.

The times shown in the following tables and recipes are examples. They will vary according to the quality, size and thickness of the meat and, of course, according to your taste.

MEATS	Quantity	Power	Cooking time	Notes
Beef Sirloin	2 portions 250g/9oz		1st side, 30secs 2nd side, 1 1/2 mins	Pre-heat the browning dish for 6 minutes. Lightly oil the meat. Brown. Allow to stand for 4 minutes. Season.
Rib of beef	800g/ 1lb12oz		1st side, 2mins 2nd side, 2mins Turn dish at 4 1/2mins	Pre-heat the browing dish for 6 minutes. Lightly oil the meat. Season 1/2 way through cooking. Allow to stand.
Steaks	300g/11oz		1st side, 1min 2nd side, 30secs	Pre-heat the browning dish for 6 minutes. Lightly oil the meat. Brown and turn after 1 minute. Season. Allow to stand after cooking.
Joints	1kg/2lb3oz		10-12 mins	Pre-heat the browning dish for 7 minutes. Lightly oil the meat. Turn and season 1/2 way through cooking. Allow to stand.

MEAT	Quantity	Power	Cooking time	Notes
Minced Beef	600g/ 1lb4oz	⊔	1st side, 30secs 2nd side, 1 1/2 mins	Pre-heat the browning dish for 6 minutes. Lightly oil the meat. Brown. Season 1/2 way through cooking. Allow to stand.
Rump Steak	500g/18oz	⊔	1st side, 1min 2nd side, 1 1/2mins	Pre-heat the browning dish for 6 mins. Lightly oil the meat. Put the steaks around the outside then turn them. Season 1/2 way through cooking. Allow to stand.
Tournados	250g/9oz	⊔	1st side, to brown 2nd side, 1min	Pre-heat the browning dish for 6 minutes. Lightly oil the meat. Put the steaks in browning dish and turn them. Season 1/2 way through cooking. Allow to stand for 3 to 4 minutes.
VEAL Escalopes	250g/9oz	⊔	1st side, 1 1/2 mins 2nd side, 1 min.	Pre-heat the browning dish for 5 minutes. Season the escalopes and oil them. Cook each side for 1 1/2 mins and 1 minute respectively. Allow to stand.
Roast	1kg/2lb3oz	⊔	22 mins	Pre-heat the browning dish for 6 minutes. Baste the joint in butter and oil. Cook uncovered for 1 min. on the 1st side to brown, 3 minutes on the second, 3 minutes on the first, 3 minutes on the second then 11 mins. Allow to stand.
Knuckle	4 slices	⊔	12 mins	Pre-heat the browning dish for 6 mins. Season and oil. Cook for 3 minutes on the 1st side, add a little butter and cook for a further 3 minutes. Turn them and cook for 6-8 minutes. Allow to stand.
PORK Ribs	300g/11oz	⊔	5mins	Pre-heat the browning dish for 5 mins. Season the ribs and lightly oil them. Cook for 2 minutes on each side. Allow to stand.
Filiets	2	⊔	10mins	Pre-heat the browning dish for 5 minutes. Cook the fillets uncovered turning them 1/2 way through cooking.
Roast	1kg/2lb3oz	⊔	24mins	Pre-heat the browning dish for 6 minutes. Lightly oil the meat. 1st side for 2 mins. 2nd side 2 mins., 1st side 2 mins. 2nd side 2 mins. Cook for 16 minutes uncovered. Allow to stand.
LAMB Ribs	400g/14oz	⊔	1st side, 1 min 45secs 2nd side, 1 1/2 mins	Pre-heat the browning dish for 6 minutes. Season the ribs and lightly oil them. Brown them on the 1st side. Turn onto the other side.
Leg (or shoulder)	1kg/2lb3oz	⊔	1st side, 3 mins 2nd side, 7mins	Pre-heat the browning dish for 5 minutes. Rub the leg with garlic and put the cloves inside. Cover and cook for 3 minutes. Turn. Turn the dish during cooking. Allow to stand for 10 minutes.

Beef balls in raisins, beer and cumin

SERVES 4

50g/2oz raisins
125ml/4fl oz water
300g/11oz pork, chopped
400g/14oz minced beef
1 size 3 egg
salt & pepper
50g/2oz flour
2 carrots, peeled, chopped
1 onion, peeled, sliced
30ml/2tbsp oil
pinch cumin grains
150ml/5fl oz pale ale
bouquet garni

METHOD

1. Soak the raisins in the water and put in the microwave for 2 minutes on power ⬛.

2. Mix the pork with the beef. Add the egg and salt and pepper. Mix well and make 8 meatballs, coat in flour.

3. Preheat the browning dish for 6 minutes on power ⬛. Add the oil and brown the meatballs on all sides. Do this in 2 sessions reheating the browning dish for 2-3 minutes on power ⬛.

4. Add the carrots, cumin, beer, raisins and bouquet garni. Cook for 8 minutes on power ⬛. Season and cook for a further 2 minutes on power ⬛.

Rumpsteak in celery and tomato

SERVES 4

1/2 stick celery, washed, sliced
25g/1oz butter
15ml/1tbsp water
425g/15oz tin tomatoes, strained
salt & pepper
15ml/1tbsp oil
2 rump steaks, 4/5cm/1 1/2-2" thick

METHOD

1. Put the celery, butter and water into a glass dish and cook for 5 minutes on power ⬛. Add the tomatoes and cook for a further 5 minutes on power ⬛. Season with salt and pepper and set aside.

2. Preheat the browning dish for 5 minutes on power ⬛. Oil the meat and brown the steak on all sides.

3. Cook for 2 1/2 minutes on each side. Salt and pepper half way through cooking. Serve with the celery.

Beefburgers

SERVES 4

225g/8oz lean minced beef
1 small onion, chopped
salt & pepper

METHOD

1. Mix the minced beef with the chopped onion and salt and pepper.

2. Divide the mixture into 4 equal portions and roll each into a ball, then flatten to form rounds about 1cm/1/2''thick.

3. Pre-heat a browning dish for 6 minutes on power , arrange the burgers on the dish.

4. Cover with a piece of kitchen paper and cook for 3 minutes, turning the meat after 1 1/2 minutes on power .

5. Serve burgers between baps with tomato slices.

Roast joints

SERVES 6

1,4kg/3lb joint of beef, lamb or pork

METHOD

1. Place the joint in a large dish, fat side down.
2. Cover with greaseproof paper and cook for 12 minutes on power ⌣.
3. Pour away surplus fat and turn joint over and cook for a further 12-15 minutes on power ⌣.
4. Cover joint in aluminium foil and leave to stand for 5 minutes to serve rare. Leave to stand for 20 minutes for a well cooked joint.
5. Brown the joint under a pre-heated grill if required.

Goulash

SERVES 4/6

700g/1 1/2lb braising steak, cubed
30ml/2 tbsp flour
salt & pepper
1 large onion, peeled, sliced
1 green pepper, deseeded, sliced
225g/8oz carrots, sliced
400g/14oz can tomatoes
75g/3oz tomato purée
75g/3oz button mushrooms
10ml/2 tsp paprika
300ml/1/2 pint beef stock

METHOD

1. Toss the meat in the flour seasoned with the salt and pepper.
2. Put the meat, onion, pepper, carrots, tomatoes, tomato purée and mushrooms into a large casserole dish.
3. Mix the paprika and beef stock together and pour over the meat. Stir well and season.
4. Cook for 40 minutes on power ⌣, stirring and turning dish during cooking.

Steak and kidney pudding

SERVES 4

25g/1oz butter
1 large onion, peeled and chopped
450g/1lb chuck steak, cubed
100g/4oz lambs kidneys, cored and chopped
25g/1oz flour
salt & pepper
5ml/1tsp mixed herbs
150ml/5fl oz beef stock
100g/4oz mushrooms, sliced

Pastry
225g/8oz S.R. flour
pinch salt
100g/4oz shredded suet
125ml/4fl oz water

METHOD

1. Place butter in a shallow dish for 45 seconds on power ᵂ.
2. Add onion and cook for a further 2 minutes.
3. Toss the steak and kidney in the flour seasoned with the salt and pepper and herbs. Add to the onions and butter mix and stir in stock.
4. Cook on power ᵂ for 3 minutes.
5. Cover with cling film and cook for 20 minutes on power ᵂ, stirring frequently.
6. Microwave on low power ᵂ for a further 15 minutes, stirring occasionally.
7. Add mushrooms, return to oven and cook for a further 2 minutes on power ᵂ.
8. Allow to cool.
9. For the pastry, mix flour, salt and suet together, add water and mix to form a soft dough.
10. Roll out, reserving 1/4 of the pastry for the lid. Line a 1 litre/1 3/4 pint pudding basin.
11. Fill with cooked meat mixture. Dampen the rim of the pie and place the pastry lid over the top, pressing the pastry edges together to seal. Make 2 or 3 slits in the pastry with a sharp knife.
12. Cover with cling film and cook on power ᵂ for 12 minutes, giving the basin a half-turn 3 or 4 times during cooking.

Beef casserole

SERVES 4

60ml/4tbsp oil
25g/1oz flour
450g/1lb chuck steak, cubed
350ml/12 fl oz beef stock
400g/14oz can tomatoes
225g/8oz onions, sliced
225g/8oz mixed vegetables
1 clove garlic, crushed
salt & pepper

METHOD

1. Blend the oil and flour in a large dish and cook for 5 minutes on power ᵂ until beige in colour.
2. Add the meat all at once, stir and cook for 5 minutes on power ᵂ, stirring after 2 minutes.
3. Add all the remaining ingredients. Cover with cling film and cook for 35 minutes on power ᵂ, stirring during cooking.
4. Leave to stand for 15 minutes before serving.

Beef with french beans

SERVES 4

400g/14oz rump steak
30ml/2 tbsp soya sauce
15g/1/2oz butter
15ml/1 tbsp oil
1 onion, peeled, sliced
500g/18oz french beans, cut in half
125ml/4 fl oz water
salt & pepper

METHOD

1. Cut the steak in strips and soak in the soya sauce.

2. Preheat the browning dish for 6 minutes on power ⬚. Add the butter and oil and add the strips of meat. Set aside.

3. Reheat the browning dish for 2-3 minutes on power ⬚, then brown the onions and french beans. Add the water, cover and cook for 7 minutes on power ⬚.

4. Add the meat, salt and pepper and cook for a further 1-2 minutes on power ⬚. Serve immediately with rice.

Beef in red wine

SERVES 4

4 rashers streaky bacon
1 large onion, peeled, chopped
450g/1lb topside of beef, cubed
15g/1/2oz cornflour
300ml/1/2 pint red wine
300ml/1/2 pint beef stock
2 cloves garlic, crushed
salt & pepper
5ml/1tsp dried thyme
100g/4oz button mushrooms, sliced
chopped parsley to garnish

METHOD

1. Cut bacon rashers into strips. Place bacon and onion in a large shallow dish and cook for 4 minutes on power ⬚.

2. Add meat and cook for a further 2 minutes on power ⬚, stirring after 1 minute.

3. Blend cornflour with a little wine in a basin. Add remaining wine, stock, garlic, seasoning and dried thyme and pour over meat mixture.

4. Return to oven and cook for 12 minutes on power ⬚, stirring every 5 minutes.

5. Add sliced mushrooms and cook for a further 3 minutes on power ⬚. Season to taste. Garnish with chopped parsley.

Shepherds pie

SERVES 4/6

1 large onion, peeled, chopped
15ml/1 tbsp tomato purée
1 beef stock cube, crumbled
300ml/1/2 pint beef stock
350g/12oz cooked minced beef
15ml/1 tbsp flour
salt & pepper
450g/1lb potatoes, peeled and cubed
60ml/4 tbsp water
15g/1/2 oz butter
25g/1oz grated cheese (optional)

METHOD

1. Place the onion, tomato purée, stock cube and stock in a large shallow dish.

2. Cover and cook for 10 minutes on power ⏰.

3. Toss the mince in the flour, then stir into the onion mixture, season well. Cover and cook for a further 10 minutes on power ⏰, stirring occasionally.

4. Place potatoes into a suitable sized dish or polythene bag, add water, seal or cover, remembering too pierce to allow steam to escape.

5. Cook for 10-12 minutes on power ⏰ until soft, turning the dish every 5 minutes.

6. Drain and mash the potatoes with the butter, adding salt and pepper to taste and the grated cheese.

7. Top mince with potato and cook for 5 minutes on power ⏰, turning every minute.

8. Place under a pre-heated grill to brown, before serving.

Pork chops in red cabbage

SERVES 4

30ml/2tbsp honey
60ml/4tbsp red wine
clove garlic, peeled, crushed
2 lean pork chops
15g/1/2oz butter
1/2 red cabbage, washed, cut into fine strips
1 apple, peeled, cored, chopped
15ml/1tbsp oil
pinch cinammon
salt & pepper

METHOD

1. Mix the honey, red wine, and garlic together and marinate the chops for at least 2 hours.

2. Put the onion in a glass dish with the butter and cook for 1 minute on power ⌣.

3. Add the cabbage, apple and the chop marinade. Cover and cook for 12 minutes on power ⌣. Set aside.

4. Preheat the browning dish for 6 minutes on power ⌣. Strain the chops, reserving the liquid.

5. Add the oil to the browning dish and brown the chops on both sides. Cook on each side for 4 minutes on power ⌣. Turn the dish during cooking.

6. Spread the cabbage around the chops, season with salt and pepper and cook for a further 2 minutes on power ⌣.

7. Serve very hot.

Roast pork with onions and potatoes

SERVES 4

800g/1lb 12oz boned loin of pork
45ml/3tbsp oil
100g/4oz onions, peeled, sliced
500g/1lb2oz potatoes, peeled, cut into strips
30ml/2tbsp milk
pinch nutmeg
salt & pepper

METHOD

1. Preheat the browning dish for 6 minutes on power ⌣.

2. Oil the meat with 30ml/2tbsp oil and brown the meat in the browning dish on all sides.

3. Cook for 5 minutes on power ⌣, then remove the meat and get rid of the juices.

4. Add the remaining oil to the browning dish, add the onions and stir well. Put in the potato strips then sprinkle with the milk and nutmeg. Place the meat in the centre of the dish.

5. Cook for 10 minutes, covered on power ⌣. Remove the cover and cook for a further 7 minutes on power ⌣.

6. Season with salt and pepper 3 minutes before the end of cooking time.

Pork chops in the browning dish

SERVES 4

4 pork chops
oil to coat
salt & pepper

METHOD

1. Dry the chops on absorbent kitchen paper.

2. Brush all the surfaces with oil.

3. Pre-heat a browning dish for 6 minutes on power .

4. Place chops into dish and cook for 1 minute on power.

5. Turn the chops over and cook for a further 2 minutes. Test chops with the tip of a sharp knife. Pork must not have any pink colour showing inside.

6. Leave to stand for 3 minutes before serving.

Caramelised roast pork

SERVES 4

75ml/5tbsp granulated sugar
30ml/2tbsp water
15ml/1tbsp oil
1kg/2lb3oz joint pork
4 onions, peeled, sliced
clove garlic, peeled, crushed
salt & pepper
30ml/2tbsp vinegar

METHOD

1. Make a brown caramel by mixing the sugar and water together (the sugar must be just wet). Cook for 3-4 minutes on power ⚏.

2. Preheat the browning dish for 5 minutes on power ⚏. Lightly oil the joint and brown it in the browning dish for 10 minutes on power ⚏.

3. Add the sliced onions and garlic, salt and pepper. Cover and cook for 15-20 minutes on power ⚏. Turn the dish during cooking.

4. Pour the caramel over the roast. Add the vinegar and cook for a further 2 minutes on power ⚏. If necessary add a little water.

Roast pork with turnips

SERVES 4

600g/1lb4oz turnips, peeled, cubed
5ml/1tsp sugar
25g/1oz butter
125ml/4fl water
30ml/2tbsp oil
800g/1lb12oz joint of pork
1 carrot, peeled, sliced
1 stick celery, washed, sliced
2 cloves garlic
salt & pepper

METHOD

1. Put the turnips, sugar, 15g/1/2oz butter and water into a glass dish. Cover and cook for 8 minutes on power ⚏. Set aside.

2. Preheat the browning dish for 6 minutes on power ⚏. Oil the joint and brown on all sides. Add the carrot, celery, garlic in their skins and remaining butter. Mix and cook for 15 minutes on power ⚏, uncovered.

3. Turn the dish during cooking, season with salt and pepper. Add the turnips and cook for 7 minutes on power ⚏. Allow to stand.

4. Garnish the turnips with chopped parsley.

Pork ribs in grapes

SERVES 4

50g/2oz butter
15ml/1tbsp oil
4 ribs of pork
300g/11oz green grapes, peeled
1/2 green pepper, chopped
salt & pepper
parsley to decorate

METHOD

1. Preheat the browning dish for 6 minutes on power ⌣. Add the 15g/1/2oz butter and the oil and brown the pork on both sides.

2. Cover and cook for 5 minutes on power ⌣. Add the grapes, green pepper, salt and pepper and remaining butter to the juices. Whisk to obtain a smooth sauce.

3. Heat for 1 minute on power ⌣, serve immediately with chopped parsley.

Chump of veal in milk

SERVES 4

**800g/1b12oz chump of veal, rolled
& tied**
200ml/7fl oz milk
45ml/3tbsp oil
2 cloves garlic, crushed
2 cloves
salt & pepper

METHOD

1. Put the meat in a glass dish with the milk, 15ml/1tbsp oil, garlic and cloves. Marinate for 24 hours.
2. Preheat the browning dish for 6 minutes on power ⌣. Strain the meat and reserve the juice. Add 30 ml/2tbsp oil and brown the meat. Cook for 10 minutes on power ⌣, remove the juices and add the reserved marinade.
3. Cook for 6 minutes on power ⌣, season and cook for a further 2 minutes on power ⌣.
4. Turn the dish during cooking. Allow to stand covered.
5. Liquidize the juices and serve very hot with the joint.

Escalopes of veal in cream and parsley

SERVES 4

1 bunch parsley, washed, plucked
1 shallot, peeled, sliced
15g/1/2oz butter
150ml/5 fl oz fresh cream
30ml/2tbsp oil
4 veal escalopes
salt & pepper

METHOD

1. Place the parsley leaves, shallot and butter in a glass dish and cook for 2 minutes on power ⌣. Add the cream and cook for a further 1 1/2 minutes on power ⌣. Liquidize and set aside.
2. Preheat the browning dish for 6 minutes on power ⌣, then add the oil. Brown the veal on both sides, then cook on each side for 2 minutes on power ⌣.
3. Season half way through cooking. Serve with the parsley and cream sauce.

Sautéed lamb with leeks

SERVES 4

40g/1 1/2oz butter
15ml/1tbsp oil
6 slices neck of lamb
2 carrots, peeled, sliced
1 onion, peeled, chopped
125ml/4fl oz water
600g/1 1/4 leeks, whites only, sliced
1 size 3 egg-yoke
juice of half a lemon
salt & pepper

METHOD

1. Preheat the browning dish for 5 minutes on power ⏣. Add 15g/1/2oz butter and the oil to the dish and brown the meat on both sides.

2. Add the carrots, onion and half the water. Cover and cook for 10 minutes on power ⏣.

3. Put the leeks into a glass bowl with the remaining butter and water and cook for 5 minutes on power ⏣.

4. Remove the cooking juices from the meat and mix with the egg yolk diluted in the lemon juice.

5. Mix all the ingredients together and season with salt and pepper. Reheat for 1 minute on power ⏣.

Lamb and courgettes with onion

SERVES 4

45ml/3tbsp oil
600g/1lb4oz shoulder of lamb, cubed
150g/5oz onions, peeled, sliced
clove garlic, peeled, crushed
500g/18oz courgettes, cubed
salt & pepper

METHOD

1. Preheat the browning dish for 6 minutes on power ⏣. Add 30ml/2tbsp oil and brown the lamb on all sides. Remove, set to one side.

2. Reheat the browning dish for 2 minutes on power ⏣. Add remaining oil, onions, garlic and courgettes. Cook for 3 minutes on power ⏣.

3. Add the cubed lamb, salt and pepper, cover and cook for 12 minutes on power ⏣. Remove the lid halfway through cooking.

Lamb curry

SERVES 4

45ml/3tbsp oil
700g/1 1/2lbs boned shoulder of
lamb
1 onion, peeled & sliced
clove garlic, peeled, sliced
1 carrot, peeled, sliced
1 leek, washed, sliced
5ml/1tsp curry powder
2.5ml/1/2tsp cinnamon
pinch cumin
pinch powdered ginger
pinch coriander
1 clove
150 ml/5fl oz natural yoghurt
bouquet garni
50ml/2fl oz water
1/2 banana, peeled, sliced
salt & pepper

METHOD

1. Preheat the browning dish for 6 minutes on power ⚟. Add 30ml/2tbsp oil to the dish and brown the meat, stirring with a wooden spoon. Set aside.

2. Reheat the browning dish for 2 minutes on power ⚟. Add 15ml/1tbsp oil and brown the onion, garlic, carrot and leek. Then add the spices. Mix together well, then pour in the yoghurt. Add the meat, bouquet garni and water.

3. Stir well, cover and cook for 8 minutes on power ⚟. Add the banana and salt and pepper and cook for a further 2 minutes on power ⚟.

4. Serve with white rice.

Sautéed lamb in fennel

SERVES 4

40g/1 1/2oz butter
15ml/1tbsp oil
600g/1lb4oz boned shoulder of lamb,
cubed
1 carrot, peeled, sliced
1 onion, peeled, sliced
700g/1 1/2lbs fennel, washed, sliced
clove garlic, peeled, crushed
5ml/1tsp curry powder
bouquet garni
50ml/2fl oz water
salt & pepper

METHOD

1. Preheat the browning dish for 6 minutes on power ⚟. Add 15g/1/2oz butter and oil to the dish, brown the meat on all sides. Remove the meat.

2. Reheat the dish for 3 minutes on power ⚟, add the meat, carrot, onion, fennel and garlic. Stir well and add the curry powder, bouquet garni and water. Cover and cook for 10 minutes on power ⚟.

3. Remove the meat and bouquet garni. Put the vegetables into a food processor to make a purée. Return to the dish and cook for 3 minutes on power ⚟. Add the remaining butter and meat.

4. Season with salt and pepper and reheat for 1 minute on power ⚟.

Shoulder of lamb in garlic and mint

SERVES 4

3 cloves garlic, peeled, crushed
8 leaves mint, chopped
30ml/2tbsp oil
600g/1lb4oz boned shoulder of lamb
salt & pepper

METHOD

1. Mix the garlic and mint together and spread this mixture over the meat. Season and tie with string.

2. Preheat the browning dish for 6 minutes on power ⏚. Add the oil and brown the shoulder on all sides.
   Cook the meat for 10 minutes on power ⏚. Season with salt and pepper.

Lamb in thyme

SERVES 4

1 boned saddle of lamb
salt & pepper
12.5ml/2 1/2tsp thyme
15ml/1tbsp oil
1 onion, peeled, chopped
1 carrot, peeled, chopped
1 stick celery, chopped
1 shallot, peeled, chopped
100ml/3 1/2fl oz water
75g/3oz butter

METHOD

1. Preheat the browning dish for 6 minutes on power ⬓.

2. Season the lamb with salt and pepper and sprinkle with 5ml/1 tsp thyme.

3. Put the lamb into the hot browning dish with the oil and vegetables. Turn the meat to brown all sides. Cover and cook for 3 minutes on power ⬓. Remove the meat and allow to stand.

4. Add the water and 5ml/1tsp thyme to the browning dish and heat for 2 minutes on power ⬓.

5. Sieve this juice into a small glass dish and add the butter and remaining thyme. Heat for 30 seconds on power ⬓, then whisk.

6. Coat the lamb with this sauce. Serve with carrots in butter.

Lamb chops

SERVES 4

4 lamb chops
4 slices lemon
1 onion, peeled, sliced
1/2 green pepper, deseeded, sliced
225g/8oz tomatoes, chopped
50ml/2fl oz beef stock
salt & pepper

METHOD

1. Place the chops in a dish with a lemon slice on top of each chop.

2. Cover chops with remaining ingredients, and season with salt and pepper.

3. Cover, and cook for 7 minutes on power ⬓. Stand for 5 minutes before serving.

Irish stew

SERVES 4

2 large onions, sliced
750g/1 1/2lb stewing lamb, cubed, fat removed
4 tomatoes, sliced
2 large potatoes, scrubbed and pricked
300ml/1/2 pint chicken stock
5ml/1 tsp dried mixed herbs
2.5ml/1/2 tsp salt
1.5ml/1/4 tsp pepper

METHOD

1. Put the onions in a large casserole dish, covered with cling film and cook for 3 minutes on power ⌣.

2. Spread the lamb over the onions and arrange sliced tomatoes on top. Cover, and cook for 10 minutes on power ⌣, stirring occasionally. Set to one side.

3. Place the potatoes on the oven shelf and cook for 5 minutes on power ⌣. Slice and arrange on top of the meat.

4. Season the stock with herbs, salt and pepper and pour over the potatoes. Cover.

5. Cook for 15 minutes on power ⌣ turning the dish once during cooking.

Ham, pork and liver

Before cooking prick black puddings or sausages with a fork to stop them bursting open.

Cook them alone or with an accompaniment.

Always turn the food and the dish during cooking.

Offal, liver, kidneys produce good results in a microwave. For the final appearance, it is better to use a browning dish.

	Quantity	Power	Cooking times	Notes
Black puddings	4	⏜	3-4 mins	Preheat the browning dish for 6 minutes. Prick the skin. Turn 1/2 way through cooking.
Sausages	4	⏜	3-4 mins	Prick the sausages. Preheat the browning dish for 6 mins.

Ham braised in pineapple

SERVES 4

25g/1oz butter
600g/1lb, 4oz ham off the bone, cut into 4 slices
4 pineapple slices
30ml/2tbsp madeira
1 onion, peeled, chopped
2 ripe tomatoes, peeled, deseeded
salt & pepper

METHOD

1. Preheat the browning dish for 6 minutes on power ⏜. Add the butter and brown the ham slices on both sides. Set aside.

2. Reheat the dish for 2 minutes on power ⏜. Add the remaining butter and brown the pineapple slices on both sides. Set aside.

3. Add the madeira, onion and tomato and cook for 2 minutes on power ⏜.

4. Add the ham and pineapple, season with salt and pepper and reheat for 1 minute on power ⏜.

Liver

SERVES 4

4 rashers bacon
15g/1/2oz butter
4 slices lambs liver
1 shallot, peeled, sliced
1 tin corn
salt & pepper

METHOD

1. Preheat the browning dish for 5 minutes on power ☜, then rapidly brown the slices of bacon on both sides. Remove them.

2. Reheat the browning dish for 3 minutes on power ☜, add the oil and butter and brown the liver slices on both sides. Remove them.

3. Add the finely sliced shallot and corn to the dish. Heat for 1 minute on power ☜.

4. Put the liver and bacon on the corn, season with salt and pepper and return to the microwave for 1 1/2 minutes on power ☜.

Vegetables

In a microwave, vegetables keep their colour, taste and nutritional qualities. Cook vegetables in a covered dish with a little butter and water — generally 30ml/2tbsp will be enough — the water can be replaced by another liquid eg. stock, wine, cider.

Be careful of the steam when removing lid.

Prick the vegetables so steam can escape. If you are cooking the vegetables whole, turn the dish during cooking. If they are cut, stir from time to time to ensure even cooking. The times shown in the following tables are examples. They will depend on the freshness, and most importantly their water content. Vegetables containing a high water content cook quickly.

Never overcook vegetables or they will dry out and harden. They will be crispy if they have a low water content (eg carrots, celery, turnips). Do not cook large quantities at one time — 500g/1lb.2oz is the best amount. It is better to add salt at the end of cooking. When removing vegetables from the microwave they will be slightly hard but will continue to cook for 3-5 minutes after being removed.

Use the browning dish for sautéed potatoes, braised celery, etc.

Cooked vegetables can be reheated without losing any flavour. Do not add water or butter. Simply cover and reheat for 1-2 minutes.

VEGETABLE	Quantity	Power	Cooking time	Notes
Artichokes	2	♨	12-15 mins	Wash, strain, cut the leaves to 1/3 of the height and cook in a covered dish with a little water.
Asparagus	1	♨	6 mins	Cook in a covered dish.
Aubergines	1	♨	6 mins	Cook in a covered dish
Cabbage	500g/ 1lb2oz	♨	10 mins	Slice the cabbage and cook with a little butter in a covered dish. Mix during cooking.
Carrots	500g/ 1lb2oz	♨	8-10 mins	Cut the carrots into thin slices. Cook in a covered dish with 30ml/2tbsp water. Add a knob of butter.
Cauliflower	500g/ 1lb2oz	♨	10-12 mins	Divide the cauliflower into bouquets. Cook in a covered dish with 45ml/3tbsp water and juice of 1/2 a lemon. Stir during cooking.

VEGETABLE	Quantity	Power	Cooking time	Notes
Celery	450g/1lb		12 mins	Finely slice the celery and cook with a knob of butter in a covered dish.
Courgettes	500g/1lb2oz		6-8 mins	Cut the courgettes into thin slices and cook in a covered dish with a little butter.
Endives	500g/ 1 1lb2oz		8-10 mins	Cut the endives into thin slices and cook in a covered dish with a little butter and a pinch of sugar, and 30ml/2tbsp water.
Fennel	500g/1lb2oz		7 mins	Cook the sliced fennel in a covered dish with a little water and 5ml/1tsp lemon juice.
French beans	500g/1lb2oz		10 mins	Cook the beans in water in a covered dish.
Leeks	500g/1lb2oz		10 mins	Slice the leeks and cook in a covered dish with 15ml/1tbsp water. Stir during cooking.
Mushrooms	500g/1lb2oz		7 mins	Cook the mushrooms with 15ml/1tbsp lemon juice, if they are small, leave them whole, if not slice them.
Peas	500g/1lb2oz		10 mins	Cook in a covered dish with 15ml/1tbsp water. Stir during cooking.
Peppers	500g/1lb2oz		6-7 mins	Cut the peppers into slices and cook in a covered dish with 15ml/1tbsp water.
Runner beans	500g/1lb2oz		6 mins	Cut the runner beans into thin slices and cook in a covered dish with a little butter and water.
Spinach	500g/1lb2oz		7 mins	Cook the spinach still wet with a little butter in a covered dish.
Tomatoes	500g/1lb2oz		3 mins	Prick the skins of the tomatoes, cook in a covered dish.
Turnips	500g/1lb2oz		10-12 mins	Cook the chopped turnips in a covered dish with a little water and a pinch of sugar.

Greek mushrooms

SERVES 4/6

15ml/1 tbsp lemon juice
100ml/3 1/2fl oz olive oil
15ml/1 tbsp tomato purée
200ml/7 oz white wine
5ml/1tsp coriander seeds
bouquet garni
clove garlic, peeled, crushed
600g/1 1/4lbs button mushrooms,
washed

METHOD

1. Pour the lemon juice, oil, tomato purée, wine, coriander seeds, bouquet garni and garlic into a glass dish and cook for 2-3 minutes on power ⬜. Stir well.

2. Add the mushrooms, salt and pepper, cover and cook for 11 minutes on power ⬜.

3. Check seasoning, remove the bouquet garni and allow to cool in the cooking juice.
Serve very cold.

Buttered mushrooms

SERVES 4

225g/8oz button mushrooms, sliced
25g/1oz butter

METHOD

1. Place mushrooms in a roasting bag with butter, tie bag loosely with string.

2. Cook for 1 1/2 minutes on power ⬜.

Buttered corn on the cob

SERVES 2

2 cobs of corn
60ml/4tbsp water
25g/1oz butter

METHOD

1. Remove husk from cobs and place in a roasting bag with the water.

2. Tie loosely with string and place in the oven for 8-10 minutes on power ⬜.

3. Remove and put on serving plate with a knob of butter on each cob.

Baked whole onions

SERVES 2

2 onions, weighing 500g/1lb

METHOD

1. Peel onions and place in a roasting bag.
2. Tie loosely with string and place in the oven for 7-8 minutes on power ⬚.

Sautéed potatoes

SERVES 4

45ml/3tbsp oil
800g/1 3/4lbs potatoes, peeled, sliced
5ml/1tsp thyme
15ml/1tbsp parsley, chopped.

METHOD

1. Preheat the browning dish for 6 minutes on power ⬚.
2. Add the oil and potatoes to brown them.
   Cook for 1 minute on power ⬚.
3. Mix the potatoes and add the thyme and parsley.
4. Cover and cook for 10 minutes on power ⬚.

Jacket potatoes

SERVES 4

4 large even sized potatoes
50g/2oz butter
salt & pepper

METHOD

1. Wash, dry and prick potatoes thoroughly.
2. Place on a double sheet of absorbent paper on the oven shelf.
3. Cook for 6 minutes on power ☕.
4. Turn the potatoes over and cook for a further 6-10 minutes on power ☕ until tender but not soft.
5. Leave to stand for 5 minutes. Split in half lenghwise and top each half with butter and salt and pepper.

Minted new potatoes

SERVES 4

450g/1lb new potatoes
75ml/3fl oz water
25g/1oz butter
5ml/1tsp freshly chopped mint
salt & pepper

METHOD

1. Scrape potatoes and place in a roasting bag with the water. Tie bag loosely with string and cook for 10 minutes on power ☕.
2. Place the butter, chopped mint, salt and pepper in a bowl and cook for 2 minutes on power ☕.
3. Transfer potatoes to a serving dish and pour over mint butter.

Cauliflower cheese

SERVES 4

1 cauliflower
600ml/1 pint boiling water
25g/1oz cornflour
300ml/1/2 pint milk
50g/2oz grated cheddar cheese
salt & pepper
15ml/1 tsp dry English mustard

METHOD

1. Cut cauliflower into florets and place in a dish. Pour boiling water over cauliflower and cook for 9 minutes on power ⌣. Drain well.

2. Blend cornflour with a little milk, add remaining milk and stir. Cook for 5 minutes on power ⌣, stirring after each minute.

3. Add half of grated cheese to sauce with salt, pepper and dry mustard, stir well and pour over cauliflower.

4. Sprinkle remaining cheese over top and place under a grill to brown.

Leeks in cheese sauce

SERVES 4

450g/1lb leeks, washed, halved
45ml/3 tbsp water
15ml/1 tbsp cornflour
225ml/8 fl oz milk
50g/2oz cheddar cheese, grated
salt & pepper

METHOD

1. Place leeks and water in a roasting bag and tie bag loosely with string. Cook for 6 minutes on power ⌣.

2. Strain, reserving liquid, and place leeks in a serving dish.

3. Blend cornflour with a little milk in a bowl, then make up to 350ml/12fl oz with reserved liquid and remaining milk.

4. Cook sauce for 6 minutes on power ⌣, stirring frequently.

5. Add half of the grated cheese, season the sauce and pour over leeks, sprinkle with remaining cheese and brown under a grill.

Stuffed peppers

SERVES 2

2 firm red or green peppers
salt & pepper
15ml/1 tbsp olive oil
15ml/1 tbsp oil
350g/12oz sausagemeat
2 crushed cloves garlic
30ml/2 tbsp tomato ketchup
pinch cayenne pepper
2 size 3 eggs, beaten

METHOD

1. Cut the peppers in half and remove the stalks and seeds.

2. Sprinkle the insides of the peppers with salt, pepper and oil, put to one side.

3. Pre-heat a browning dish for 5 minutes on power 🍳.

4. Add the oil and sausagemeat, turning the sausagemeat to brown sides. Cook for 6 minutes on power 🍳.

5. Add remaining ingredients to the browned sausagemeat and blend together.

6. Fill pepper halves with sausagemeat and place them in a shallow dish and cook for 10 minutes on power 🍳, turning the dish after 5 minutes. Allow to stand for 5 minutes before serving.

Stuffed tomatoes

SERVES 4

150ml/5fl oz milk
100g/4oz rice, cooked
45ml/3tbsp oil
1 onion, peeled, chopped
2 cloves of garlic, peeled, crushed
30ml/2tbsp chopped parsley
200g/7oz sausagemeat
1 size 3 egg
pinch nutmeg
salt & pepper
4 large tomatoes

METHOD

1. Heat the milk in a bowl for 1 minute on power 🍳, then soak the rice. Crush well with a fork and remove excess liquid. Set aside.

2. Add 15ml/1tbsp oil to the dish and brown the onion, garlic and parsley for 1 minute on power 🍳. Add the sausagemeat and cook for a further minute on power 🍳.

3. Add the rice, egg, nutmeg and salt and pepper.

4. Prick the tomato skins with a fork. Remove the top part of the tomatoes which will form the lid. Scrape out the pulp and keep aside.

5. Divide the filling into 4 and stuff each tomato. Place them in the dish with their lids on.

6. Add the remaining oil and the tomato pulp to the dish. Cover and cook for 8-10 minutes on power 🍳. Turn the dish during cooking.

Stuffed cabbage

SERVES 4

1 small green cabbage, washed, leaves separated
75ml/3fl oz water
salt & pepper
1 onion, peeled, chopped
1 shallot, peeled, chopped
clove garlic, peeled, chopped
15g/1/2oz butter
200g/7oz minced beef
1 size 3 egg yolk
5ml/1tsp parsley, chopped
5ml/1tsp mint, chopped
1 tomato, skinned, deseeded
juice of a lemon

METHOD

1. Put the cabbage leaves in a glass dish with the water and salt and pepper. Cook for 2 minutes on power ☐, then run cold water over them and sponge dry.

2. Put the onion, shallot, garlic and butter in a glass dish. Cover and cook for 3 minutes on power ☐. Mix with the meat, egg yolk, parsley, mint and cabbage leaves too small to be stuffed, which should also be chopped.

3. Season and mix well. Make small balls of stuffing and roll the cabbage leaves around the balls.

4. Arrange the stuffed cabbage in a glass dish, add the tomato pulp and the lemon juice.

5. Cover and cook for 8 minutes on power ☐.

Buttered parsnips

SERVES 4

450g/1lb parsnips, peeled, sliced
25g/1oz butter
5ml/1 tsp dried thyme
salt & pepper

METHOD

1. Place parsnips in a roasting bag with the butter and thyme and tie loosely with string.
2. Cook for 10 minutes on power ⍛. Season before serving.

Buttered broccoli

SERVES 4

450g/1lb broccoli
45ml/3 tbsp water
salt & pepper
25g/1oz butter

METHOD

1. Place broccoli in a roasting bag with the water and tie bag loosely with string.
2. Cook for 7 minutes on power ⍛.
3. Place in a serving dish, season and add butter.

Braised celery

SERVES 4

25g/1oz butter
1 carrot, peeled, diced
1 head celery, washed, cut into
4cm 1 1/2 " pieces
60ml/4tbsp chicken stock
salt & pepper

METHOD

1. In a large dish, melt butter for 45 seconds on power ⍛.
2. Add carrot and celery and cook for 2 minutes on power ⍛.
3. Pour over stock, cover with cling and cook for 15 minutes on power ⍛.
4. Season with salt and pepper.

Mixed vegetables

SERVES 4

50g/2oz butter
45ml/3tbsp water
100g/4oz carrots, peeled, diced
100g/4oz turnips, peeled, diced
100g/4oz swede, peeled, diced
100g/4oz corn
100g/4oz peas
salt & pepper

METHOD

1. Melt the butter in a large bowl for 45 seconds on power ♨.

2. Add the water, carrots, turnips, swede and cook for 10 minutes on power ♨. Stir well.

3. Add the corn, peas and season with salt and pepper. Cook for a further 5 minutes on power ♨, until the vegetables are tender.

Carrots in raisins

SERVES 4

800g/1lb.12oz carrots, peeled, cut
into strips
1 onion, peeled, sliced
15g/1/2oz butter
50g/2oz raisins
salt & pepper

METHOD

1. Put the carrots and onion in a bowl with the butter and cook for 2 minutes on power ⌣.

2. Add the raisins, cover and cook for 10 minutes on power ⌣. Season with salt and pepper at the end of cooking.

Ratatouille

SERVES 2

30ml/2tbsp oil
1 medium onion, peeled, chopped
2 cloves garlic, crushed
1 medium green pepper, sliced
225g/8oz courgettes, sliced
225g/8oz aubergines, sliced
175g/6oz tomatoes, quartered
pinch cayenne pepper
bouquet garni
salt & pepper

METHOD

1. Place the oil, onion, garlic and green pepper in a bowl. Cover with cling film and pierce the top.

2. Cook for 3 minutes on power ⌣.

3. Add the courgettes and aubergines and cook for a further 7 minutes on power ⌣.

4. Add remaining ingredients, seasoning to taste and cook for 4 minutes on power ⌣.

Pasta and rice

Microwaves do not cook pasta much quicker than when cooking by the traditional method, but do have much better results when reheating.

Pasta and rice keep their flavour and their texture, they do not stick and do not need fat added.

Pasta can easily be cooked in advance and then reheated just before serving.

	Quantity	Power	Cooking times	Notes
PASTA	250g/9oz	☵	6 mins	Put the pasta in 1 litre/1 3/4 pt hot water, add salt and 30ml/2tbsp oil. Cover and allow to cook. Stir during cooking. Allow to stand for 6 mins.
RICE	250g/9oz	☵	10 mins	Cook in a covered dish with 1 litre/1 3/4 pints boiling water with salt and oil. Allow to stand for 10 mins.

Remember to use large dishes as pasta/rice increase in volume when cooked.

Tagliatelle

SERVES 4

600ml/1 pint boiling water
2.5ml/1/2 tsp oil
pinch salt
225g/8oz tagliatelle
125ml/4fl oz cream
50g/2oz emmenthal cheese, grated
50g/2oz cooked garlic sausage, sliced
salt & pepper

METHOD

1. Pour boiling water into a large deep dish, add the oil and salt, and gently lower in the tagliatelle.

2. Stir once and cook uncovered for 6 minutes on power ☵ until just beginning to soften.

3. Cover tightly and leave to stand for 10 minutes.

4. Drain the tagliatelle.

5. Place the cream, cheese, garlic sausage and seasoning in a small bowl.

6. Heat for 3 minutes on power ☵ until the cheese melts. Stir well.

7. Add the cream mixture to the tagliatelle and mix together well. Serve immediately.

Risotto

SERVES 4

30ml/2tbsp oil,
1 onion, peeled, chopped,
200g/7oz rice,
5ml/1tsp tomato purée,
2 tomatoes, peeled, crushed, strained,
1 thick slice of cooked ham, chopped,
100g/4oz cheddar cheese, cubed,
salt & pepper,
chives to garnish.

METHOD

1. Preheat the browning dish for 5 minutes on power ⏻. Add the oil and brown the onion and the rice.

2. When the rice has turned an ivory colour pour twice its volume in water into the dish with the tomato purée.

3. Cover and cook for 15 minutes on power ⏻.

4. Add the ham, cheese, salt and pepper and cook for 3 minutes on power ⏻.

5. Garnish with chives and serve hot with lemon juice.

Macaroni cheese

SERVES 2

100g/4oz macaroni
600ml/1 pint boiling water
5ml/1tsp salt
15g/1/2oz butter
25g/1oz flour
5ml/1tsp mustard
300ml/1/2 pint milk
100g/4oz grated cheddar cheese
pepper
tomato slices to garnish

METHOD

1. Place macaroni in a bowl. Pour over boiling water and add salt.
2. Cook for 5 minutes on power 🍲.
3. Melt butter in a bowl for 45 seconds on power 🍲. Stir in the flour and mustard.
4. Gradually add the milk, whisking all the time.
5. Cook for 3-4 minutes on power 🍲 whisking frequently, until the sauce thickens.
6. Drain the macaroni and stir into the sauce with grated cheese. Add seasoning to taste.
7. Garnish with tomato slices.

Spaghetti

SERVES 4

600ml/1 pint boiling water
2.5/1/2tsp oil
salt
225g/8oz spaghetti

METHOD

1. Pour boiling water into a large deep dish, add the oil and salt and gently lower in the spaghetti.
2. Stir once and cook without covering for 6-7 minutes on power 🍲 until just beginning to soften.
3. Cover tightly and leave to stand for 10 minutes.
4. Drain the spaghetti throughly and serve.

Sauces

Apple sauce

450g/1lb cooking apples, peeled cored and sliced
30ml/2tbsp water
15ml/1tbsp caster sugar

METHOD

1. Place apples and water in a suitable dish and cover with cling film. Cook for 8 minutes on power ⌣.

2. Mash apples to a pulp and stir in sugar. Serve as required.

Custard

15ml/1tbsp custard powder
15ml/1tbsp sugar
300ml/1/2 pint milk

METHOD

1. Mix custard powder and sugar together in a large basin. Blend in a little of the milk and mix to a smooth paste.

2. Add remaining milk and stir. Cook for 2 minutes on power ⌣, remove and stir.

3. Return to oven for a further 3 minutes on power ⌣ until custard is thick. Remove and stir.

Basic white sauce

25g/1oz butter
25g/1oz plain flour
300ml/1/2 pint milk
salt & pepper

METHOD

1. Melt butter in a jug by heating for 45 seconds on power ⌣.

2. Stir in the flour and add the milk gradually, stirring all the time.

3. Heat on power ⌣ for 3 minutes, whisking every minute to keep sauce smooth. Season.

Mornay sauce

25g/1oz butter
25g/1oz flour
300ml/1/2 pint milk
1 egg yolk
50g/2oz cheese, grated
salt & pepper

METHOD

1. Melt butter in a jug by heating for 45 seconds on power ⌣.

2. Stir in the flour and add the milk gradually, stirring all the time.

3. Heat on power ⌣ for 1 minute. Whisk and heat for a further minute. Whisk again to keep sauce smooth.

4. Cook for 1 minute on power ⌣, and then add the egg yolk, seasoning and cheese and whisk until the cheese is dissolved.

Hollandaise sauce

100g/4oz butter
2 size 3 egg yolks
strained juice of 1 small lemon
1.5ml/1/4tsp dry mustard
1.5ml/1/4tsp salt

METHOD

1. Melt butter in a jug by heating for 1 minute on power ⏚.
2. Beat the egg yolks with the lemon juice, mustard and salt.
3. Whisk the egg mixture into the melted butter. Cook for 1 minute on power ⏚, stirring after 30 seconds.

Parsley sauce

25g/1oz butter
25g/1oz plain flour
300ml/1/2 pint milk
10ml/2tsp chopped parsley
salt & pepper

METHOD

1. Melt butter in a jug by heating for 45 seconds on power ⏚.
2. Stir in the flour and add the milk gradually, stirring all the time.
3. Heat on power ⏚ for 2 minutes. Whisking every minute to keep the sauce smooth.
4. Add the chopped parsley and seasoning. Cook for a further minute on power ⏚.

Bearnaise sauce

2 shallots, peeled, chopped
50ml/2fl oz wine vinegar
30ml/2tbsp chopped tarragon
salt & pepper
100g/4oz butter
2 size 3 egg yolks

METHOD

1. Put the shallots in a small dish with the vinegar, tarragon and salt and pepper.
2. Heat uncovered for 3 minutes on power ⏚, then sieve.
3. Put the strained liquid in a dish and add knobs of butter. Heat for 30 seconds on power ⏚ and whisk.
4. Beat in the egg yolks and heat for 30 seconds on power ⏚.

Butter in white wine sauce

3 shallots, peeled, chopped
50ml/2fl oz vinegar
salt & pepper
100g/4oz butter

METHOD

1. Put the shallots in a glass dish with the vinegar, salt and pepper. Cook uncovered for 3 minutes on power ⏚, then sieve.
2. Add knobs of butter and cook for a further 30 seconds on power ⏚, then whip.
3. You can make a butter and red wine sauce by replacing the vinegar with red wine.

Tomato sauce

500g/18oz fresh, ripe tomatoes, washed,
1 onion, peeled, sliced
clove of garlic, peeled, crushed
15ml/1tbsp oil
1 sprig of thyme
30ml/2tbsp chopped parsley
salt & pepper

METHOD

1. Put the tomatoes in the microwave for 1 minute on power ⌣, so they are easier to peel. Remove the pips and crush the flesh.

2. Put the onion and garlic in a glass dish with the oil and cook for 2 minutes on power ⌣, add the tomatoes, thyme, half the parsley and cook for 6 minutes on power ⌣. Season after 3 minutes.

3. Stir during cooking. At the end of cooking add the rest of the parsley.

Mushroom sauce

250g/9oz button mushrooms, sliced
juice 1/2 a lemon
15g/1/2 oz butter
125ml/4fl oz cream
30ml/2tbsp chives, chopped

METHOD

1. Put the mushrooms into a glass dish with the lemon juice, butter and water.

2. Cover and cook for 5 minutes on power ⌣.

3. Season and add the fresh cream. Mix well and cook for 3 minutes on power ⌣. Before serving add the chopped chives.

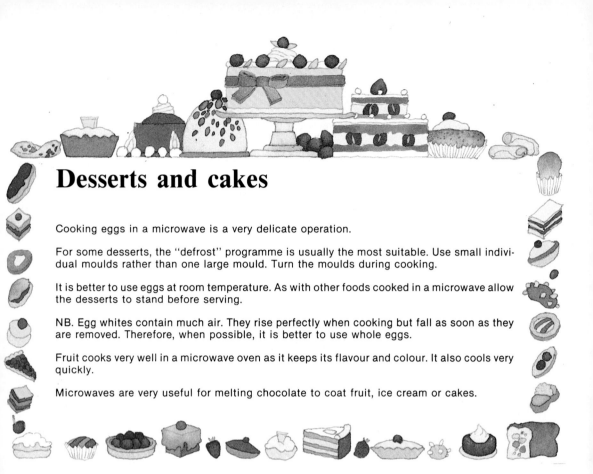

Desserts and cakes

Cooking eggs in a microwave is a very delicate operation.

For some desserts, the "defrost" programme is usually the most suitable. Use small individual moulds rather than one large mould. Turn the moulds during cooking.

It is better to use eggs at room temperature. As with other foods cooked in a microwave allow the desserts to stand before serving.

NB. Egg whites contain much air. They rise perfectly when cooking but fall as soon as they are removed. Therefore, when possible, it is better to use whole eggs.

Fruit cooks very well in a microwave oven as it keeps its flavour and colour. It also cools very quickly.

Microwaves are very useful for melting chocolate to coat fruit, ice cream or cakes.

Rhubard ramekins in strawberry sauce

SERVES 4

200g/7oz rhubarb, washed, sliced
100g/4oz caster sugar
200g/7oz creamed cheese
75ml/3fl oz cream
1 size 3 egg and egg yolk
15g/1/2oz flour

Strawberry sauce :
200g/7oz strawberries, puréed
30ml/2tbsp caster sugar
juice half a lemon

METHOD

1. Place the rhubarb in a glass dish with the sugar. Cook for 4 minutes on power 🕛. Then put into a food processor to make a purée.

2. Add the cream cheese, cream, egg, egg yolk and flour. Mix well.

3. Pour this mixture into individual dishes and cook for 3 minutes on defrost setting 🕛. Cook for a further 3 minutes on power 🕛.

4. Turn the dishes during cooking to ensure even cooking. Allow to cool.

5. Mix the strawberry purée, sugar and lemon juice together.

6. Put the ramekins and sauce in a cool place before serving.

Chocolate ice cream

SERVES 4

200ml/7fl oz water
75g/3oz caster sugar
juice 1/2 a lemon
200g/7oz plain chocolate
15ml/1tbsp fresh cream

METHOD

1. Pour the water into a measuring jug and add the sugar and lemon juice.
2. Cook for 3 minutes on power ⏝.
3. Break the chocolate into pieces and put into a glass dish, cover and melt for 2 minutes on power ⏝.
4. With a hand whisk add the sugar mix to the chocolate. Mix well and add the fresh cream.
5. Pour into a container and place in the refrigerator.

Cream cheese flan

SERVES 4

2 size 3 eggs and 1 yolk
150g/5oz caster sugar
500g/1lb2oz cream cheese
peel of 1 lemon
50g/2oz SR flour
50g/2oz raisins

METHOD

1. Mix the eggs and sugar in a large bowl, and add the cream cheese, lemon peel, flour and raisins.
2. Mix together well and pour into a buttered 20cm/8" tart mould. Cook for 6 minutes on power ⏝.
3. Serve cold in the mould. The flan can be served with stewed fruit eg cherries.

Floating island

SERVES 4

275ml/1/2 pt milk
5ml/1tsp vanilla essence
3 size 3 eggs
50g/2oz granulated sugar
50g/2oz pink praline

Syrup :
100g/4oz granulated sugar
30ml/2tbsp water
4 drops lemon juice

METHOD

1. Heat the milk with the vanilla essence for 2 1/2 minutes on power 🍲.

2. Break the eggs and separate the white from the yolk. Beat the yolks with the sugar until it forms a white mixture. Then pour the warmed milk into the mixture, whisking all the time.

3. Cook for 1 minute on power 🍲, whisk and put back for a further minute on power 🍲. Pour straightaway into a serving dish. (If the cream turns lumpy during cooking blend it in a food processor.

4. Grind the praline in a liquidizer until it forms a powder.

5. Make a syrup with the sugar, water and lemon juice in a measuring jug. Cook for 2 minutes on power 🍲.

6. Whisk the egg whites to a stiff snow, then pour the praline into the syrup. Stir into the egg whites. Cook for 15 seconds on power 🍲.

7. Butter a soufflé mould, add the egg whites pressing firmly, refrigerate.

8. Remove the island from the mould by sliding it onto a plate.

9. So as not to break "the island" slide it into the centre of the cream, from the plate.

10. Garnish with the praline and serve cold.

Three flavoured ice cream

SERVES 4

575ml/1pt milk
50g/2oz chocolate
15ml/1tbsp water
6 size 3 eggs
75g/3oz caster sugar
10ml/1tsp coffee extract

METHOD

1. Heat the milk in a measuring jug for 2 minutes on power ⌣.
2. Place the chocolate and water in a bowl and melt on power ⌣ for 1 minute.
3. Beat the eggs and sugar and vanilla essence together in a large bowl. Add the warmed milk slowly and mix well. Divide mixture into three.
4. Add coffee to one part, chocolate to another, the third remains vanilla.
5. Turn the dishes during cooking and allow to cool before serving.

Baked jam pudding

SERVES 4

45ml/3tbsp jam
175g/6oz SR flour
75g/3oz margarine
75g/3oz caster sugar
grated peel 1 lemon
2 size 3 eggs
45 ml/3tbsp milk

METHOD

1. Grease a large pudding bowl 1.1 litre/2 pint with a little butter, spread jam over bottom of the bowl.
2. In another bowl sift flour and rub in margarine finely. Add sugar and lemon peel.
3. Combine with eggs and milk to make a soft batter ; DO NOT BEAT.
4. When batter is smooth, pour over jam.
5. Cook uncovered, for 7 minutes on power ⌣, or until well risen, turning twice ; at this stage the top should look slightly wet.
6. Leave to rest for 5 minutes before serving.
7. The jam can be substituted with 45ml/3tbsp golden syrup.

Baked apples

SERVES 4

4 medium sized cooking apples
40g/1 1/2oz butter
50g/2oz soft brown sugar
25g/1oz raisins
30ml/2tbsp chopped nuts
50ml/2fl oz water
15ml/1tbsp thin honey

METHOD

1. Wash and core the apples and cut a slit around the centre of each.
2. Put the butter, sugar, raisins, and nuts in a bowl and mix well.
3. Divide and fill the apple cavities with the stuffing mix and place in a large dish.
4. Mix the water and honey together and spoon over the apples. Cover the apples with greaseproof paper.
5. Cook for 6-8 minutes on power ⚕ until tender.

Apricot flan

SERVES 6

25g/1oz butter
150ml/5fl oz milk
3 size 3 eggs
100g/4oz granulated sugar
50g/2oz SR flour
350g/12oz tinned apricots, strained
25g/1oz flaked almonds

METHOD

1. Put the butter in a glass bowl and melt for 45 seconds on power ⏛. Add the milk, eggs, sugar and flour and mix well until you get a smooth cream.

2. Butter the tart mould, and put the apricot halves in the mould with the uncut edge on the outside. Pour in the mixture and garnish with the flaked almonds.

3. Cook for 8 minutes on defrost setting ⏛ then 4 minutes on power ⏛. Turn the mould during cooking.

4. Serve hot or cold. You can replace the apricots with other fruit eg. cherries, plums, prunes, peaches.

Cheesecake

SERVES 4

75g/3oz butter
200g/7oz digestive biscuits, crushed
450g/1lb soft cream cheese
75g/3oz caster sugar
2 size 3 eggs
10ml/2tsp vanilla essence

METHOD

1. Melt butter in bowl for 2 minutes on power ⏛. Combine with biscuit crumbs, and press mixture into the base of a 25cm/10" fluted flan dish.

2. Whisk the cream cheese, sugar, eggs and vanilla essence together until smooth.

3. Pour over crumb base and cook for 12 minutes on power ⏛, turning dish a quarter turn every 3 minutes.

4. Leave to cool, then refrigerate for 1 hour before serving.

5. Top cheesecake with any variety of topping i.e. pie filling, fresh fruit etc.

Scones

225g/8oz plain flour
pinch salt
10ml/2tsp baking powder
50g/2oz butter
25g/1oz caster sugar
25g/1oz sultanas
1 size 3 egg, beaten
75ml/5tbsp milk

METHOD

1. Sift the flour, salt and baking powder into a large bowl and rub in the butter until the mixture resembles fine breadcrumbs.

2. Add the sugar and sultanas. Stir in the egg and milk and mix to form a smooth soft dough which drops from a spoon.

3. Shape the dough into a ball then flatten to form a round about 1cm/1/2" thick. Cut into 3cm/1 1/2" rounds. Place on non stick paper in the oven, spacing them well apart.

4. Cook for 3 1/2 minutes on power ⏛, moving the scones around every minute. Insert a skewer into the centre of each scone, if it comes out clean the scones are cooked. Any uncooked scones can be cooked for a further 30 seconds on power ⏛.

5. Brown tops of scones under a grill.

Orange cake

3 size 3 eggs
175g/6oz caster sugar
175g/6oz butter
rind and juice 1 orange
50g/2oz ground almonds
75g/3oz SR flour, sieved
5ml/1tsp yeast, dried

Decoration :
15ml/1tbsp redcurrant jelly
orange slices
strawberries

METHOD

1. Line a 20cm/8'' cake mould with buttered greaseproof paper.

2. Whisk the eggs and sugar together in a large bowl until light and fluffy.

3. Melt the butter in a glass bowl for 45 seconds on power ⏳.

4. Gently fold into the whisked mixture the melted butter, orange rind and juice, ground almonds, flour and yeast.

5. Mix together well then pour mixture into the prepared cake mould. Cook for 6 minutes on power ⏳, turning the cake during cooking.

6. Allow to stand for 5 minutes and loosen the mould under the grill. Allow to cool.

7. Put the redcurrant jelly in a bowl and melt for 1 minute on power ⏳. Brush the melted jelly over the cake and decorate with orange slices and strawberries.

Date and nut cake

150g/5oz butter
3 size 3 eggs
75g/3oz brown sugar
5ml/1tsp vanilla essence
100g/4oz SR flour, sieved
5ml/1tsp dried yeast
12 dates, chopped
25g/1oz ground almonds
40g/1 1/2oz walnuts, chopped
15ml/1tbsp honey

METHOD

1. Line a 20cm/8" cake mould with buttered greaseproof paper.

2. Put the butter in a glass bowl and melt for 45 seconds on power ⬚.

3. Whisk the eggs and sugar together in a large bowl, then add the melted butter, vanilla essence, flour, yeast, dates, ground almonds, walnuts.

4. Mix together well and pour into the prepared cake mould. Cook for 6 minutes on power ⬚, turning the cake during cooking.

5. Allow to stand for 5 minutes then loosen the mould under the grill. Allow to cool.

6. Melt the honey for 45 seconds on power ⬚ then coat the cake using a brush.

Lemon and coconut cake

150g/5oz butter
3 size 3 eggs
75g/3oz brown sugar
75g/3oz caster sugar
rind and juice 1 lemon
25g/1oz dessicated coconut
100g/4oz SR flour
5ml/1tsp dried yeast
grated coconut

METHOD

1. Line a 20cm/8" cake mould with buttered greaseproof paper.

2. Melt butter in a bowl for 45 seconds on power ⬚.

3. Whisk the eggs and sugars together in a large bowl until light and fluffy. Gently fold in the melted butter, lemon rind and juice, coconut, flour and yeast.

4. Mix quickly and pour into the cake mould. Cook for 6 minutes on power ⬚, turning the cake during cooking.

5. Allow to stand for 5 minutes in the mould then loosen under the grill. Allow to cool. Serve sprinkled with coconut.

Chocolate and nut cake

100g/4oz plain chocolate
15ml/1tbsp water
100g/4oz butter
3 size 3 eggs
100g/4oz caster sugar
50m/2fl oz milk
50g/2oz wheat flour
5ml/1tsp dried yeast
50g/2oz walnuts, chopped

Decoration :
15ml/1tbsp redcurrant jelly
walnuts

METHOD

1. Break the chocolate into a bowl, add the water and melt for 2 minutes on power ⏚.

2. Add the butter and heat for 1 minute on power ⏚. Mix well with a metal whisk.

3. Line a 20cm/8" cake mould with buttered greaseproof paper.

4. Whisk the eggs and sugar together in a large bowl until light and fluffy.

5. Add the milk, chocolate, flour, yeast and nuts. Mix together with a whisk, pour into the cake mould.

6. Cook for 6 minutes on power ⏚, turning the cake during cooking.

7. Allow to stand for 5 minutes, then loosen under the grill.

8. Melt the redcurrant jelly in a bowl for 1 minute on power ⏚, then coat the cake. Decorate with walnuts.

Christmas pudding

SERVES 4

225g/8oz mixed fruit
25g/1oz glace cherries, chopped
1 small cooking apple, peeled, cored chopped
25g/1oz candied peel, chopped
40g/1 1/2oz chopped almonds
grated rind of 1 lemon
grated rind and juice 1 small orange
50g/2oz plain flour
1.5ml/1/4tsp salt
1.5ml/1/4tsp mixed spice
1.5ml/1/4tsp ground cinnamon
1.5ml/1/4tsp grated nutmeg
50g/2oz dark brown sugar
25g/1oz fresh breadcrumbs
50g/2oz shredded suet
75ml/3fl oz brandy
15ml/1tbsp black treacle
2 size 3 eggs, beaten
milk as necessary

METHOD

1. Mix together all the fruit, peel, nuts, grated rind and juice in a large bowl.
2. Sift the flour, salt and spices together.
3. Add the sugar, breadcrumbs and suet to the fruit.
4. Mix well, then stir in the remaining ingredients, adding just enough milk to form a mixture which will easily drop from a spoon.
5. Turn the mixture into a greased 1 litre/1 1/3 pint pudding basin.
6. Cover with cling film and cook for 8 minutes on power ⏳.
7. Leave to stand for a few hours.
8. To re-heat cook for 2-3 minutes on power ⏳.

Marble cake

175g/6oz butter
3 size 3 eggs
175g/6oz caster sugar
50ml/2fl oz milk
100g/4oz SR flour, sieved
5ml/1tsp yeast, dried
25g/1oz cocoa powder, sieved

METHOD

1. Line a 20cm/8" cake mould with buttered greaseproof paper.
2. Melt the butter in a glass bowl for 45 seconds on power ⏳.
3. Whisk the eggs and sugar together in a large bowl until light and fluffy. Then gently fold in the melted butter, milk, flour and yeast.
4. Mix together well, then divide the mixture into two. Add the cocoa powder to one half.
5. Pour into the cake mould, in sequence, one layer of cocoa mixture, then 1 layer of vanilla. Start and finish with the cocoa to colour the cake.
6. Cook for 6 minutes on power ⏳, turning the cake during cooking.
7. Allow the cake to stand for 5 minutes, then loosen the mould under the grill.
8. Either sprinkle icing sugar over the cake or cover it with chocolate coating. For the chocolate coating melt pieces of chocolate in a bowl for 2 minutes on power ⏳. Whisk to smooth paste. Coat the cake and allow to cool.

Soda bread

225g/8oz plain flour
225g/8oz wholemeal flour
30ml/2tbsp baking powder
5ml/1tsp salt
50g/2oz butter
300ml/1/2 pint milk
5ml/1tsp vinegar
30ml/2tbsp black treacle
few porridge oats

METHOD

1. Sift the flours, baking powder and salt together in a large bowl.

2. Rub in the butter until completely incorporated and make a well in centre of mixture.

3. Put the milk, vinegar and black treacle into a jug and cook for 30 seconds on power ⏛.

4. Pour into the flour and mix together for 1-2 minutes.

5. Knead until the mixture is smooth on a lightly floured surface. Then shape into a 15cm/6" round. Sprinkle top of bread with porridge oats and mark a deep cross on top of the loaf.

6. Cover a plate with greaseproof paper and place bread on top.

7. Cook for 6 minutes on power ⏛ giving the plate a quarter turn every 1 1/2 minutes.

8. Test by inserting a skewer through the loaf, if it comes out clean the loaf is ready. If necessary cook for a further minute on power ⏛.

Spicy bread

200g/7oz plain flour, sieved
100g/4oz caster sugar
5ml/1tsp ground aniseed
5ml/1tsp cinammon
50g/2oz butter
200ml/7fl oz milk
100g/4oz honey
5ml/1tsp dried yeast

METHOD

1. Line a 20cm/8" cake mould with buttered greaseproof paper.

2. Place the flour, sugar, aniseed powder, and cinammon into a large bowl.

3. Melt the butter in a bowl for 45 seconds on power ⏛.

4. Warm the milk for 1 minute on power ⏛, then add the honey and melted butter.

5. Pour the liquid mixture into the flour and mix quickly, pour into the cake mould.

6. Cook for 6 minutes on power ⏛.

7. Allow to stand for 5 minutes then loosen mould under a grill.

Flapjacks

75g/3oz butter
75g/3oz soft brown sugar
100g/4oz porridge oats

METHOD

1. Put the butter into a 18cm/7" round shallow dish and cook for 1 minute on power ⏛ until melted.

2. Stir in the sugar and oats and mix thoroughly. Press down evenly into dish.

3. Cook for 4-5 minutes on power ⏛ until a skewer inserted into the centre comes out clean. Turn the dish a quarter turn every minute during cooking.

4. Cut into wedges straightaway. Leave to cool until firm and turn out onto a wire rack.

Confectionery

Caramels

100g/4oz plain chocolate
100g/4oz granulated sugar
100g/4oz butter
100g/4oz honey

Optional 25g/1oz chopped hazelnuts

METHOD

1. Put the pieces of chocolate, sugar, butter and honey in a glass bowl.
2. Cover and cook for 2 minutes on power ⏣.
3. Mix with a whisk and cook for 3 minutes on power ⏣, stirring every minute : the last time add the nuts.
4. Pour the mixture into a buttered mould and allow to cool.
5. Cut into squares.

Fruity fudge

25g/1oz butter
225g/8oz granulated sugar
75ml/5tbsp condensed milk
60ml/4tbsp water
2.5ml/1/2tsp vanilla essence
50g/2oz sultanas

METHOD

1. Lightly grease a small rectangular dish.
2. Put the butter into a large bowl and melt on power ⏣ for 30 seconds.
3. Stir in the sugar, milk, water and vanilla essence and continue stirring well until the sugar is almost dissolved.
4. Cook for 2 minutes on power ⏣, then give the bowl a gentle shake.
5. Cook for a further 6 minutes on power ⏣.
6. Remove bowl from oven and quickly beat in sultanas and continue beating the mixture until it is thick and creamy and tiny crystals form. Once the crystals form stop beating.
7. Pour the fudge quickly into the prepared dish. Allow to cool and keep for 24 hours in the refrigerator. Turn out and cut into squares.

Chutneys, jams and marmalades

It is advisable only to make small quantities of jam that can be eaten within a few weeks following their preparation. For larger quantities it is better to prepare jam by the traditionnal method.

Fruit chutney

4 plums, stoned, chopped
2 apples, peeled, cored, chopped
2 pears, peeled, cored, chopped
5ml/1tsp powdered ginger
2 cloves garlic, peeled, crushed
15ml/1tbsp raisins
15ml/1tbsp vinegar
pinch paprika
1 clove
pinch cinammon
salt & pepper

METHOD

1. Put all the ingredients into a large bowl and mix together well.
2. Cook for 10 minutes on power ♨, stirring often.
3. Allow to cool and serve with a curry.

Tomato chutney

450g/1lb onions, finely chopped
1.8kg/4lb tomatoes, skinned and chopped
300ml/1/2 pint malt vinegar
275g/10oz granulated sugar,
15g/1/2oz salt
15ml/1tsp cayenne pepper
25g/1oz dry mustard
15ml/1tbsp allspice wrapped in muslin

METHOD

1. Place onions, tomatoes, vinegar, sugar and salt into a large bowl, stir well.
2. Cover and cook for 10 minutes on power ♨, turning bowl every five minutes.
3. Uncover and mix in cayenne pepper and mustard. Place allspice wrapped in muslin cloth into the chutney.
4. Cook for a further minute on power ♨.
5. Remove muslin bag and allow chutney to cool. Pot and cover.

Strawberry jam

Makes 500g/1lb2oz jam

500g/1lb2oz strawberries, washed,
400g/14oz granulated sugar,
juice of half a lemon.

Put the strawberries, sugar and lemon juice into a bowl. Mix carefully.

Cook uncovered for 12-14 minutes on power ⏛. Stir after 5 minutes to dissolve the sugar.

Pour into sterilized jam jars and allow to cool. Cover with cling film.

Apple, pear and grape jam

Makes 500g/1lb2oz jam

300g/11oz apples, cut into pieces
200g/7oz pears, cut into pieces
50g/2oz grapes
400g/14oz granulated sugar

METHOD

1. Put the apples, pears, grapes and sugar into a large bowl and mix well.
2. Cook uncovered for 14 minutes on power ⏚.
3. Pour into sterilized jam jars and allow to cool. Cover with cling film.

Cherry marmalade

Makes 500g/1lb2oz jam

500g/1lb2oz cherries, stoned
400g/14oz granulated sugar
pinch cinammon

METHOD

1. Put the cherries, sugar and cinammon into a large bowl. Mix carefully and cook uncovered for 15 minutes on power ⏚.
2. Shake the dish and turn it from time to time to ensure even cooking.
3. Pour into sterilized jam jars and allow to cool. Cover with cling film.

Lemon curd

Makes 900g/2lbs

4 large lemons, grated
4 size 3 eggs, beaten
225g/8oz caster sugar
100g/4oz unsalted butter, cubed

METHOD

1. Place the grated lemon rind into a 2.8 litre/5pint mixing bowl.
2. Squeeze the juice from the lemons and add to the beaten eggs. Strain into the bowl.
3. Stir in the sugar, then add the butter. Cook for 6 minutes on power ⏚. Whisking every minute to avoid curdling.
4. When the lemon curd is thick remove from the microwave and whisk until the mixture is cool.
5. Pot in sterilised hot jars, cover and store in the refrigerator. Makes 900g/2lbs.

Hot Drinks

Russian Tea

Put 5ml/1tsp tea and 200ml/7fl oz water in a mug. Heat for 2 minutes on power ♨, then allow to draw for 5 minutes. Sieve and serve with a slice of lemon.

Grog

Put 5ml/1tsp honey, 125ml/4fl oz water and 50ml/2fl oz rum in a mug. Heat for 1 1/2 minute on power ♨ and serve.

Mulled Wine

Put 10ml/2tsp sugar and 200ml/7fl oz red wine in a mug. Add a clove and a small stick of cinammon. Heat for 1 1/2 minute on power ♨. Serve with a slice of orange.

Cocoa

Melt 25g/1oz chocolate in a mug. Add 100ml/3 1/2fl oz milk. Mix well and add a further 100ml/3 1/2fl oz milk and 5ml/1tsp coffee. Stir well and heat for 1 minute on power ♨.
Serve with a little fresh cream.

Irish Coffee

Put 75ml/5tbsp Irish whiskey and 10ml/2tsp sugar in a mug. Heat for 45 seconds on power ♨. Stir and top up mug with water. Add 10ml/2tsp coffee. Heat for 1 1/4 minutes on power ♨. Cover with cream poured over the back of a spoon.

Milk Punch

Heat 200ml/7fl oz milk with 30ml/2tbsp rum in a mug for 45 seconds on power ♨. Add a little grated nutmeg sprinkled on top.

Gin Grog

Put 150ml/5fl oz water, juice 1/2 lemon, 5ml/1tsp honey and 1 clove in a mug. Heat for 1 1/2 minute on power ♨. Add 30ml/2tbsp gin and serve.

Hot Chocolate

Put 15ml/1tbsp cocoa, 5ml/1tsp sugar and 200ml/7fl oz milk into a bowl. Mix well and heat for 1 minute on power ♨. Add a little grated orange peel and pinch of cinammon.

Coffee

Put 5ml/1tsp coffee in a mug. Top up with 200ml/7fl oz milk. Mix well and heat for 1 1/2 minute on power ♨.

Index

Produced by :   **TÉLÉCUISINE**
Recipe Testing : **Bernard et Christine Charretton**
                    Jane Massey
Photography : **Jean-Louis Roulier — Télécuisine Dimson**
Illustrations : **Michèle Trumel**

Aubin Imprimeur
LIGUGÉ, POITIERS

Achevé d'imprimer en novembre 1987
Nᵒ d'impression P 25646
Dépôt légal novembre 1987
Imprimé en France